The Anatomy of
True Christianity

The Anatomy of True Christianity

WHAT SAITH THE SCRIPTURE?

N. Jerome McClain Sr.

Copyright © 2012 by N. Jerome McClain Sr.

Library of Congress Control Number: 2012910853
ISBN: Hardcover   978-1-4771-2966-1
         Softcover   978-1-4771-2965-4
         Ebook   978-1-4771-2967-8

All rights reserved. No part of this book may be reproduced or transmitted in any form or by any means, electronic or mechanical, including photocopying, recording, or by any information storage and retrieval system, without permission in writing from the copyright owner.

This book was printed in the United States of America.

To order additional copies of this book, contact:
Xlibris Corporation
1-888-795-4274
www.Xlibris.com
Orders@Xlibris.com
110528

TABLE OF CONTENTS

Think About It!	vii
Foreword	ix
Preface	xi
What the Bible doesn't say	1
Salvation	3
Church Ordinances	19
Baptism	21
Communion	31
Substantiations	35
Ritualization vs. Realization	39
Stewardship	43
Tithing	49
Offerings	57
The Church	59
Church Administration	63
Eschatology	69
Epilog	117
Index	123

THINK ABOUT IT!

Fact: As sure as you are born you are going to die.
Fact: After death comes the judgment.
Fact: If there is no God and you are not saved, you will be okay.
Fact: If there is a God and you are not saved, you will be in Hell forever!
Fact: If there is a God and you are saved, you will be in Heaven forever!
So, What in Hell is worth Dying For?

NOTHING!

For all that is in the world, the lust of the flesh, and the lust of the eyes, and the pride of life, is not of the Father, but is of the world. 1 John 2:16

But every man is tempted, when he is drawn away of his own lust, and enticed. Then when lust hath conceived, it bringeth forth sin: and sin, when it is finished, bringeth forth death. James 1:14-15

Figure 1 Time to Decide.

FOREWORD

A friend in the ministry once shared with me that he rushed to the beach one morning to see the sun rise. As he took in this great sight the Spirit of God spoke to him asking him "What do you see?" He replied, "I see the sun rising." The Spirit replied "No, look again. What do you see?" His answer was the same, to which the Spirit restated the same question. This dialog continued until my friend finally got it. The sun was not rising. The sun is a constant and remains in its position. The earth is moving, rotating on its axis, not the sun. Although, we all refer to this event as "sun rise" the fact remains that that terminology is not correct. Pastor McClain deals with a similar presupposition that relates to Christianity, that is, the idea that one has to qualify "Christian" with "born again". It should be well understood that being a Christian means having been born again. Pastor McClain unpacks this truth one layer at a time, supporting each layer with a Scriptural foundation.

Pastor McClain expounds on the symbolism behind the church ordinances of baptism and communion and the role that each play in Christianity. In this book Nat McClain embraces Jesus' charge to those who sought Him after He had fed the multitude. Jesus charged *"Ye seek me, not because ye saw* (sought to understand the source of) *the miracles, but because ye did eat of the loaves, and were filled."* After further dialog regarding their understanding of the "bread" Jesus declared *"Moses gave you not that bread from heaven; but my Father giveth you the true bread from heaven. For the bread of God is he which cometh down from heaven, and giveth life unto the world."* (John 6:26-33)

As we can see, once again the people had embraced symbols and pictures and missed the true meaning behind it. Pastor McClain very skillfully points out that neither baptism nor communion adds anything to salvation, but are symbolic pictures that allows one to peek into the spiritual realm and gain valuable understanding relating to the Believer's position in Christ and relationship to the Father through Christ, that could not otherwise be understood in the physical realm.

The subject matter of Stewardship as it relates to money and finances has either been misunderstood and miscommunicated or totally ignored by church leadership. Pastor McClain believes that whatever authority that the church exercises in the discipline of stewardship must be supported by the Scriptures. Therefore, he uses the Scriptures to answer questions that many struggle with today such as: Is tithing Old Testament or is it for today? Does God have a purpose for giving? These questions and others like them are answered in this book.

Being a pastor for many years himself, Nat McClain adds to the field of pastoral care a dimension of wisdom and insight that is very much needed for both pastors and church members. Members, new and well seasoned will benefit greatly as Pastor McClain biblically defines the church and its origin and gives a brief yet very informative overview of the major church administrations and highlights their differences.

Essential to living a victorious Christian life is knowing that you were once lost and having responded to God's gift of salvation, you are now saved and secure in Christ Jesus, who will one day return for each Believer and take them to the place the He has prepared. The chapter in this book dealing with Eschatology, the study of end times and final events on the earth, is so compelling that I sincerely doubt if one can read it without literally praising the Lord for the victory that is already won.

This work is not based solely on the results of extensive research nor does it result from notes on some laboratory experiment, but rather principles that Pastor McClain has used in his own ministry for years, with great results I might add. I highly recommend this work to those having a desire for the sincere milk of the Word. Pastor McClain's approach to those who ask "What saith the Scriptures?" is "Let the bible speak".

Thomas L. Staples,
Pastor, &
Commandant, Jesus Cadets (JDETS), Troop 100, Jacksonville, Florida

PREFACE

What is the purpose of the Church? Does it have a mission? If it does, how many honest, insightful Christians would agree that as a rule, that mission is being carried out? Without a doubt, the *Church* is the living body of our Lord and Saviour; however *churchanity* is a powerful satanic tool used to confuse Christians and inhibit the full use of God's gifts. This book will help you to distinguish between the two. It will direct you through the fundamentals of being in the true Church of God. The bible admonishes us to be diligent observers of the truth. How can we, who admittedly do not know as much as our teacher, gauge those whom we have assumed to be anointed? The answer is in the word, "agreement". *"Can two walk together, except they be agreed?"* (*Amos* 3:3) For example, you know beyond a shadow of a doubt who Jesus is, but your teacher represents Him as someone else. Should you continue to sit under this teacher? When it is a foregone conclusion that essential bible doctrines are not embraced by your teacher, it's time to find another church.

More often than not, pastors opt to focus on non-salvational and even unscriptural opinions and in doing so leave members without appropriate doctrination, development and conditioning. We have digressed to a system of fleshly approval rather than spiritual reality. Sadly enough, the masses have grown accustomed to leaving church having obtained no foundational truths.[1] Teachers who do not teach the fact that Jesus is the only way, the truth, and the life, and who do not profess the certainty and permanence of salvation, shed a bad light on Christianity. Such teaching weakens the believer and causes one to question their own salvation which in turn can prevent them from the ultimate benefits of being saved. We are incapable

---

1   Jeremiah 5:31

of sharing that which we do not have an abundance of. And so is the ironic plight of faithful church goers who attend to be replenished, but end up being depleted instead. *"The thief cometh not, but for to steal, and to kill, and to destroy: I am come that they might have life, and that they might have it more abundantly. (John 10:10)* This is a serious epidemic within the Church.

The bible is full of information and instructions concerning heaven, yet religious leaders stagnate around futile, carnal topics concerning this world which is passing away. Sermons promoting self-righteousness and prosperity are preferred over more important matters like faith, love, and hope. Having an understanding of these areas eliminates many of the crippling doubts that Christians encounter and will help them become powerful witnesses. It is time for believers to resist being caught up in churchanity's emotional rollercoaster that is completely devoid of scriptural and spiritual substance. Being preoccupied in the sensationalism of church is a leading cause of spiritual blindness. Rigid hold to the sacred cows of tradition, that again, have no spiritual foundation, is another. While believers are fixated on inconsequential matters, they neglect personal bible study and are unaware that they are being controlled by leadership with the unsound teachings of critical doctrines. *" Having a form of godliness, but denying the power thereof: from such turn away. For of this sort are they which creep into houses, and lead captive silly women laden with sins, led away with divers lusts, Ever learning, and never able to come to the knowledge of the truth. (2 Timothy 3:5-7)*

The topic of salvation is a good example of how important doctrines can be grossly misconstrued. Loyal congregants are confused about how to become saved and whether or not their salvation is secured. Such confusion serves as a means of control rather than as a way of freeing the Lord's flock. The truth is that when you accept Jesus as your Lord and Saviour, the judgment of sin's penalty has been eternally removed. *"We know that whosoever is born of God sinneth not; but he that is begotten of God keepeth himself, and that wicked one toucheth him not. (1 John 5:18)* In spite of this and a plethora of other scriptures demonstrating everlasting salvation, countless pastors insist that once procured, a believer has the responsibility of maintaining salvation with their own good behavior. What a blatant disregard for the sacrifice our Lord and Savior Jesus made on our behalf. *"And I give unto them eternal life; and they shall never perish, neither shall any man pluck them out of my hand." (John 10:28)*

True wisdom is imputed by the Holy Spirit through our consistent obedience to the study of God's word. *"As newborn babes, desire the sincere milk of the word, that ye may grow thereby."* (1 Peter 2:2) We are the church because we are saved, not because we are trying to be saved. We attend church to be fed God's word, which empowers us to do His will. It is through agreement that we walk together but salvation is the work of Jesus alone. Remember a car broken down on the side of the road is still a car. Although it may be incapacitated for a moment, it is still known by its' maker. Don't let your journey be afflicted with the many crippling opinions which contradict and conflict with the truth. Jesus was never concerned about the interpretations of the religious order of His day. He tirelessly confronted them with the truth. So, why today should any believer be concerned with the blatantly unscriptural opinions of others? The prophetic book of Jeremiah succinctly sums up the phenomenon:

The prophets prophesy falsely, and the priests bear rule by their means; and my people love to have it so: and what will ye do in the end thereof?
Jeremiah 5:31

With your bible in hand and the Holy Spirit in heart, examine this book with the question "What saith the scripture?"

NJM

WHAT THE BIBLE DOESN'T SAY
Moments with the bible: Gospel series #102

God does not say, "Whosoever is moral, respectable, honest, well spoken of, and an office-holder or member of the church will be saved." This is man's first false way of salvation-- character. It was the Pharisee's way—"God, I thank Thee that I am not as other men."And so he "trusted in himself." (see Luke 18:9,11) Was he "justified," cleansed of his sins? No (verse 14). Why not? Because he was only righteous in his own sight, and in the sight of those around him. In God's sight he was a sinner, for "all have sinned." When it comes to man's character, there is no difference"(Romans 3:22,23). In God's sight, "there is none righteous, no, not one" (Romans 3:10), and God is the Judge.

God also does not say, "Whosoever does good works will be saved." This is man's second false way of salvation—works. Did it ever strike you—what good works can a sinner do? As is the tree, so is its fruit; as is the man, so are his works. If you are a sinner, your works are sinful and of no merit for salvation. "But we are all as an unclean thing, and all our righteousness's are as filthy rags" (Isaiah 64:6). Thus, you see, a sinner can't do any works that please God. Even more than that, my unsaved friend, in God's sight you are a sinner and therefore "dead in trespasses and sins" (Ephesians 2:1). Now, what can dead people do? Nothing! It is life you need, and it is life God offers you.

Does God ask you as a sinner to work for salvation? No, His Word declares that salvation is "not of works" (Ephesians 2:9). Galatians 2:16 tells us three times that salvation is not by works, and three times that it is by faith. Read that verse—it leaves no doubt!

Finally, God does not say "Whosoever has a certain feeling is saved." This is man's third false way of salvation—feelings. This is a common mistake with anxious souls. "Oh," says one, "if only I could feel some new feeling within me, I think I would be all right." You think so, but does God say so? Never. He does not ask you to feel, but to believe His word and trust His Son.

I know what you want. You want to feel "the joy of salvation." But how can you feel the joy of salvation, until you first have salvation? A drowning man can't feel the joy of being saved until first he is saved, and neither can you. Likewise, just as feeling can't save him, neither can it save you. Salvation is a fact, not a feeling, and rests on these three great facts—Christ died for our sins, He was buried, and He has risen again (1 Corinthians 15:3,4).[2]

---

[2] *Taken from Moments With the Book "For God So Loved the World" – Gospel Series #102*

SALVATION

The need for salvation is evidenced by the fact that we are all born in sin and the wages of sin is death. Every human being is infected with an <u>A</u>cquired <u>I</u>mmune <u>D</u>eficiency <u>S</u>yndrome (AIDS). Our only hope for survival lies in Jesus' sacrifice.[3]

> *For the wages of sin is death; but the gift of God is eternal life through Jesus Christ our Lord.*   Romans 6:23

The purpose of this book is to help you to recognize and claim God's saving power through the manifestation of Jesus the Christ. Being "saved" or "born again" simply refers to a person having acknowledged Jesus Christ as their personal Lord and Saviour. It involves *becoming* something rather than *doing* something.[4]

The third chapter of St. John discusses the difference between *doing* something to be saved and *becoming* something to be saved. It reveals the emptiness of religion and the fullness of faith in Christ Jesus. There was a sect of Jews known as Pharisees who were religious and very powerful. "Pharisees were at various times a political party, a social movement, and a school of thought among Jews during the Second Temple period beginning under the Hasmonean dynasty (140–37 BCE) in the wake of the Maccabean Revolt."[5] Nicodemus was among this elite sect and also held a high ranking political office as a ruler of the Jews. He came to Jesus by night; apparently seeking spiritual truth which he presumed would be helpful in teaching

---

3   Romans 5:20
4   John 3:3, 5, 1John 5:1-5
5   From Wikipedia, the free encyclopedia

God's word. That he was already religious is a foregone fact, proven by his position and membership in the sect of Pharisees. His conduct with respect to tangible acts must have been beyond reproach. Jesus confounded this influential teacher when He affirmed that "except a man be born again he cannot see the kingdom of God".[6] For Nicodemus, salvation was a matter of rituals consisting of laws and conduct. When Nicodemus heard the words "born again" he logically thought that Jesus was referring to being born again physically. Jesus continued to explain that before being able to enter the kingdom of God you must be able to see it. Seeing the kingdom requires spiritual eyes.

Jesus emphasized to Nicodemus the concept of "born of water" and "born of the Spirit" with these terms: "verily, verily", "except", and "must be". Many have determined the discourse between Jesus and Nicodemus to mean that you must be baptized of water and born of the Spirit to see the Kingdom of God. If we understand "born of water" to mean being baptized, then the thief's entry with Christ supersedes this important doctrine.[7] Another interpretation could be that Christ was only relating to Nicodemus individually; maybe Nicodemus needed to be baptized. This would be highly unlikely since the orthodox Jew did not have to be baptized as did the proselytes (those converted from the Gentiles). This would also imply that Christ was saying that the water cleanses us from sin. This assumption is altogether unscriptural.

An even more careful examination of John chapter three reveals two distinct existences. The first is the fleshly existence (the first Adam existence). The second is the spiritual existence (the last Adam existence).[8] The Lord admonished Nicodemus that although he was a master of earthly things he was yet ignorant of spiritual things.[9] Nicodemus' lack of spiritual insight made it impossible for him to grasp the concept of a person being miraculously and invisibly transformed into a spiritual being. Christ was simply revealing to Nicodemus that his initial existence was of flesh, and that if he desired to inherit God's kingdom it would be imperative that he undergo the new birth.[10] No flesh shall inherit the Kingdom of God.[11] "God is a Spirit and

---

6   John 3:3
7   Luke 23:42,43
8   ^{3} 1 Corinthians 15:45
9   John 3:10
10 John 3:6
11 ^{5} 1 Corinthians 15:50

we must worship Him in Spirit and in Truth."[12] Now we begin to see the meaning of the terms; *born again, re-birth, regenerated, and born of the Spirit.* We are born flesh, but must be born again spiritually. Jesus was not discussing the ordinances of the Church, but the way of salvation.

The process of salvation can be compared to physical birth. There was a phase in our human development called gestation. Gestation is the development of the embryo inside of the mother that eventually leads to live birth. There are normally three stages of three month periods called trimesters. During this period the child is growing to a point of being born alive with all the faculties of human existence. As new born babes we were overwhelmed by the power of our senses. It was only through the use and development of those senses that we acquired the ability to maneuver independently. We then learned to respond to our surroundings intelligently. Obviously, the child is human due to birth and not due to conduct. Conduct will certainly become a requirement for certain accomplishments but it does not determine humanity. The same is true for salvation; conduct is a by-product not a determinant; an effect, not a cause.

It is God's desire that all mankind become saved through spiritual re-birth. The True Church (all Christians) is the earthily vessel that God has empowered for the purpose of sharing His word thereby facilitating the re-birth of newcomers.[13] As the caretaker, the church can be seen as a "mother" giving birth to new spirit creatures. The difference between the actual and the figurative "church" mother is that the physical child must learn its birthday from his mother whereas the spiritual child must be the one who informs its mother when it has become re-born spiritually.

Jesus is God!

After being given dominion of the world, man surrendered it to Satan through sin.[14] Because humanity willfully relinquished ownership, a ransom of redemption would now be required to redeem all that God had given man dominion over. The ransom itself required a perfect redeemer; anything less than perfect would have been insufficient. So God determined for Himself a physical body through which He would make the ultimate sacrifice of

---

12 John 4:24
13 Acts 2:47
14 Revelation 5:2

redemption for humankind. Since we have all sinned and fallen short of God's glory, where else could a perfect human being come from?[15] This could and would only be possible with God. The First Epistle of John (5:6) references Jesus' required birth and death.[16] The water marks His human birth and life, the blood marks His death. Because God is just, He paid for what Adam lost rather than simply taking it back. It wasn't until after His resurrection did Jesus proclaim that "all power is given unto me in heaven *and* in earth".[17] Make no mistake about it, God is our redeemer and He purchased us with His own blood.[18]

Many argue that God cannot die therefore, Jesus could not possibly be God. This has caused many to deny the deity of Christ. In spite of the glaring indications of God's humanity in the Scripture they refuse to acknowledge Him. The bible speaks of the blood of God, which He used to purchase the Church.[19] We all agree that God is a Spirit.[20] Without a doubt, a Spirit having blood is inconsistent with the bible's description of spirit.[21] In Revelation chapter one verses four and five, we are able to see that the Church is purchased with the blood of Jesus. Just as the scripture in Revelation represents Jesus as being the One "that loved us", it also represents God the Father in John 3:16. Were there two bloods (Father and Son) or one God that saved us? Jesus' message of His deity was destined to be preached:

> "And without controversy great is the mystery of godliness: **God was manifest in the flesh**, justified in the Spirit, seen of angels, preached unto the Gentiles, believed on in the world, received up into glory." 1 Timothy 3:16

Consider Jesus' name.[22] The name Jesus means "Savior of His people". The

---

15   Romans 3:23
16   1John 5:6
17   Matthew 28:18
18   Acts 20:28
19   Acts 20:28 Take heed therefore unto yourselves, and to all the flock, over the which the Holy Ghost hath made you overseers, to feed the church of God, which he hath purchased with his own blood.
20   John 4:24 God is a Spirit: and they that worship him must worship him in spirit and in truth.
21   1 Corinthians 15:50 Now this I say, brethren, that flesh and blood cannot inherit the kingdom of God; neither doth corruption inherit incorruption.
22   Matthew 1::21

Saviour of the people, by necessity, must be a member of the human race yet without sin. Because all men are born guilty of sin there was a need for God to become man so that the penalty of perfect blood could be paid. Jesus, the child that was born to save the world, was destined by the name Emmanuel, which by interpretation is "God with us." Although the Scripture states explicitly that His name would be called Emmanuel, nowhere else in the Scripture is it used as a means of getting Christ's attention. The name was not given to the people as a means of addressing the Lord; it was given as a means of acknowledging Him. Jesus is the child Emmanuel; therefore He is "God with us".

Sin

Satan is the author of sin which explains why sin can be defined as anything that separates us from God, thereby resulting in death. There are three distinct characteristics of sin that we will refer to as the three P's: presence, power, and penalty.

Temptation is the proof of sin's presence. Where there is no attraction there can be no temptation, thus temptation is another word for lust. Eve became attracted to the Tree of Knowledge by her senses and she began to look at it lustfully. Once a person has become attracted to sin, all of their faculties become engaged. Compare these two verses below for their agreement concerning sin:

> *And when the woman saw that the tree was good for food, and that it was pleasant to the eyes, and a tree to be desired to make one wise, she took of the fruit thereof, and did eat, and gave also unto her husband with her; and he did eat.*   Genesis 3:6

> *For all that is in the world, the lust of the flesh, and the lust of the eyes, and the pride of life, is not of the Father, but is of the world.*   1 John 2:16

The tree was good for food; lust of the flesh. It was pleasant to the sight; lust of the eyes. The tree was desirable for making one wise; pride of life. Keep in mind that the reason sin causes death is that it creates separation from God. God is life and in Him is nothing that surrenders to death. God's only limitation is His absolute power. He cannot be anything less than God. The instant sin is acquired, death becomes inescapable.

Sin may be likened unto a five hundred pound weight lying on the chest of a man. If the man is dead he will not know that the weight is there. If the man is alive he will not only be aware that the weight is there, but will do everything in his power to remove it. Because this weight is sin, the man is powerless to remove it on his own. Because of the crushing power of the weight, death is its ultimate result. Although all men are burdened by the weight of sin, some will refuse to acknowledge its existence. Interestingly, such ones often live a life of ease and comfort.[23] This is possible since the weight is relative to spiritual life and is not an actual weight. However, if it is not lifted the person dies and their cozy abode on earth will be replaced with eternal torment. On the other hand, those of us who acknowledge the Lord have received a new birth endowed by the Spirit of God. The new birth gives us the power to overcome the ultimate devastation which is eternal damnation.[24] The weight of sin, even for the believer, will eventually render separation of the soul from the flesh, i.e. death, but thanks to God, our next destination is His home to receive a glorified body.[25] Becoming aware of sin's weight is the initiation of repentance for those who respond by asking God for relief.

Death is not a philosophy, it is a reality. All humans must depart from this earth; the destiny of some will be heaven, while hell will be the destination for the others. The greatest question on earth is, "are you going to heaven or hell?" The decision must be made prior to departure from the flesh.[26] Damnation is avoidable only through salvation.[27] At the moment you receive the new birth, you receive eternal life and therefore the damnation of sin is removed. You are still subject to the lust of the presence of sin (temptations) and to the consequences of the power of sin (physical death), but thanks to God, your salvation is secure.

---

23 Luke 16:19 There was a certain rich man, which was clothed in purple and fine linen, and fared sumptuously every day:
24 John 5:29 And shall come forth; they that have done good, unto the resurrection of life; and they that have done evil, unto the resurrection of damnation.
25 John 14:2-3 In my Father's house are many mansions: if it were not so, I would have told you. I go to prepare a place for you. And if I go and prepare a place for you, I will come again, and receive you unto myself; that where I am, there ye may be also.
Luke 16:22 And it came to pass, that the beggar died, and was carried by the angels into Abraham's bosom: the rich man also died, and was buried;
26 John 3:18 John 9:4
27 Matthew 18:8, 25:46, 2Thessalonians 1:9 2Peter 2:9

Repentance

Repentance is a change of thought to correct a wrong and gain ~~~ from the person who is wronged. In the sight of God we are all sinners a.. therefore separated from Him. Because we are incapable of living a sinless life we would be doomed without the opportunity to become a new and acceptable creature. Our *repentance* acknowledges these facts and seeks the unmerited favor of *mercy* and *grace*, which renders us *justified*.

Repentance then, is the first step in the process of salvation because it is the awareness that divine salvation is necessary.[28] *Belief* that Jesus is the Christ (the manifestation of God in the flesh[29]) is also absolutely essential to spiritual gestation. The potential convert must acknowledge this fact. Then, and only then, can one become saved. *Conversion* is the act of trusting God to deliver one through the process of salvation thereby making the *regeneration* possible.

Conversion/Regeneration

Now that we know *what* must happen, let's try to examine *how* it happens. We said earlier that we must first recognize our sinful plight in order to respond. Every human being possesses a competent soul allowing for the appropriate response to the call of Jesus.

> *The individual, because he is created in the image of God, is responsible for his moral and religious decisions. He is competent under the leadership of the Holy Spirit to make his own response to God's call in the gospel of Christ, to commune with God, and to grow in the grace and knowledge of our Lord. With his competence is linked the responsibility to seek the truth and, having found it, to act upon it and to share it with others. While there can properly be no coercion in religion, the Christian is never free to be neutral in matters of conscience and conviction.*[30]

---

28 [1] Matthew 3:2; Luke 13:13
29 1Timothy 3:16
30 ©Copyright 1998 C.B Hastings
Text was scanned and OCRed from <u>Introducing Southern Baptist</u> ©Paulist, Press 1981.
ISBN: 0-8091-2364-9
Library of Congress Number: 81-80052

This means that you are born with the necessary provisions to attain salvation. The Apostle Paul emphasized this competency even among the gentiles:

> (For not the hearers of the law are just before God, but the doers of the law shall be justified. For when the Gentiles, which have not the law, do by nature the things contained in the law, these, having not the law, are a law unto themselves: Which shew the work of the law written in their hearts, their conscience also bearing witness, and their thoughts the mean while accusing or else excusing one another;) Romans 2:13-15

SPIRITUAL COMPETENCY OF THE SOUL

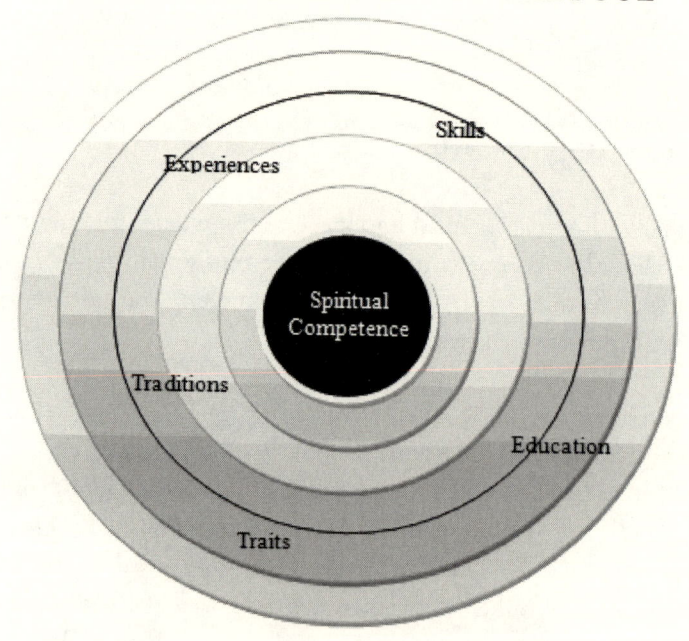

Figure 2 Spiritual Competence of the Soul

The outer circles of the above illustration represent the many layers of academic and cultural developments that must be permeated before the revealing of our inner self (*children are innocent of these layers and are considered worthy of God's kingdom*[31]). The word of God chips away at the layers that would otherwise prevent us from seeing and knowing the things that God

---
31 Matthew 18:2-4

has given us to accomplish through His will. Remember, you are not working to be saved; you are working because you are saved.[32]

We are born with unique gifts, skills and insights.[33] The Lord requires dividends from these spiritual talents. These gifts are designed for His acknowledgement and purpose, alone. We will be judged for our works or lack of works, however this is not in conflict with once saved, always saved.[34] A Christian bears two judgments: The first is that of sin, for which we are judged as being the guilty sinners we are, but have our sentence of damnation suspended by the grace of God when we become saved. The second is the Bema judgment which takes place in heaven where every believer will be judged for the works they did, or neglected to do, while here on earth. The value of a Christian's works begins only after their salvation has been secured. God judges works according to our own individual abilities given us by Him. Too often, people base their spiritual productivity on the perceivable works of another person, giving no consideration to the gifts and limitations given them by God. Such consideration omits the reality that their own calling is likely completely unique to that of someone else. If you find yourself in such a circumstance, rest assured that God has not yet communicated your calling to you.

There is nothing that you can do to modify your talents, they were predetermined by God.[35] Just as you are not able to add an inch to your height, the same limitation applies to your spiritual gifts. Most of us will never reach our pre-determined spiritual potential and this reality will be the basis for the Bema judgment.

I remember coming to the reality that the ship I was captain of was destined to nowhere except hell. Of course, or off course, how would I get anywhere else? I have never been to heaven. Therefore, I confessed my inadequacy, my ignorance, my degeneracy and my emptiness. This was my point of conversion. I received God's love letter to me. In it, I found the map to heaven and an accomplished Captain who had made the journey often, and was daily vectoring souls into heaven. I turned to Him by His will and my submission, and He turned me to Himself by *His* love and *His* power. This union equipped me with all that is needed for the journey to heaven. When

---

32   Philippians 2:12
33   Matthew 25:15
34   I Corinthians 3:13-15
35   Matthew 25:15 And unto one he gave five talents, to another two, and to another one; to every man according to his several ability; and straightway took his journey.

I turned to Him I was converted. When He turned to me I was regenerated. Simply put, I was born again.

At that moment, I was set aside for the Lord; experientially sanctified. This is the point in development where true life begins. We start as babes in Christ. We continue in the state of experiential sanctification while growing *in* this world, but not *of* this world.[36] We develop in holiness and righteousness at the hand of God. We learn obedience at the hand of the Holy Ghost and our relationship is secure with the Father through Jesus. The bible is the schoolmaster that brings us unto the Faith.[37]

> "*Ask* (Regenerated-Faith) *and it shall be given, seek* (Sanctified-Hope) *and ye shall find, knock* (Glorified-Charity) *and the door* (Righteousness-Holiness) *will be opened unto you.*"   Matthew 7:7

This one verse covers the whole election principle.[38] This is "The process by which God Regenerates, Sanctifies and Glorifies." Each phase in the plan of salvation presupposes the phase prior to it. When we enter by asking, it is appropriate to conclude by faith, that we will be glorified. God gives the increase, we only claim it. We will develop in the areas of Faith, Hope, Charity, Righteousness and Holiness, relative to our obedience in the Word of God.

Look at Salvation through Trifocals.

1. *God the Father gives us daily that which we stand in need of.*[39]
2. *God the Son forgives us of our past.*[40]
3. *God the Holy Ghost protects our future.*[41]

This is not to say that we have three Gods. This identifies the three distinct personas of the one true God who alone exhibits infallibility, immutability, perfection and absolute power.[42] Our need for salvation is apparent in our inherent weakness and can only be fulfilled by His strength and ability to be

---

36　John 17:14-16
37　Galatians 3:24
38　Ephesians 1:4; 1 Peter 1:2
39　Matthew 6:11
40　Matthew 6:12
41　Matthew 6:13
42　Romans 1:20

both just and justifier.[43] Think of it, were it not for the security provided by the Almighty Power of God no sinner would have any prospect of attaining eternal life. But because of His saving grace, salvation is not just possible, it is assured.[44]

Sanctification

Sanctification is the act or process of acquiring sanctity, of being made or becoming holy. To sanctify is literally "to set apart for special use or purpose", figuratively, "to make holy or sacred". It is the process by which the believer is developed and delivered to the very presence of God.

When a lost soul becomes saved, it is no surprise to our omniscient Creator. The bible makes it perfectly clear that God knew you before you were conceived. This being true, God foreknew that you would become saved long before the notion even entered your mind. Remember that all the time leading up to your re-birth was simply your spiritual gestation period. In gestation, from God's standpoint, you were already in a state of *Positional Sanctification* which means you were unknowingly being prepared for your re-birth. Having become saved, you entered into the *Experiential Sanctification* stage of your spiritual life because you became acutely aware of your salvation and of the lost state from whence you were delivered. In the *Experiential Sanctification* stage, you are also now privy to the third and final phase of your spiritual life when you will become *Ultimate Positional Sanctified*. This phase occurs after your physical death of which the bible teaches that to be absent from the body is to be present with the Lord. In short, when the soul embraces the Spirit of God you are experientially sanctified; this is your spiritual re-birth. When the soul of a saint separates from the body, it is ushered into the very home of almighty God; this is the state of ultimate positional sanctification. These three phases can also be referred to as regeneration, sanctification, and glorification respectively.

Eternal Salvation

There is seldom a denial of the effectiveness of a person's confession on their dying bed. Most teachers, regardless of their take on whether or not salvation

---

43 Romans 3:26
44 John 10:28; Philippians 1:6; Romans 8:33-39; 1 Corinthians 3:15; 1 John 5:10-11

can be lost, will agree that the "dying declaration of salvation" is effectual. When an individual dies immediately after having accepted Jesus as their Lord and Saviour, most readily believe the deceased to be in heaven. The salvation that the person receives on his/her death bed is no different than the salvation received by someone who has many years remaining on earth. The only difference is the fact that the person on earth is encumbered with the presence of sin whereas the person who dies immediately after is not. Having said this, do we really believe that the person who died immediately after being saved would not have sinned again if their life had been prolonged? Certainly not! So, when people represent an apparent sin as evidence that a person is not saved, they are incorrectly representing salvation as something achieved by works.

The behavior most readily associated with salvation can be seen in most of the world's religions since high standards of morality are not exclusive to Christians. Some of the most moral people in the world are Buddhists, Muslims, and even Atheist. Of a truth, Christianity is often rejected by non-believers on the grounds that Christians do not adequately represent moral excellence. The idea that morality represents being saved is unscriptural.

"For by grace are ye saved through faith; and that not of yourselves: it is the gift of God: Not of works, lest any man should boast."
Ephesians 2:8-9

In spite of this passage, countless Christians diminish our Saviors' sacrifice by attributing salvation to works. The suggestion is that Christ's sacrifice is not sufficient to save and must be contributed to by our own perfect works. How preposterous! Becoming saved in no way rehabilitates Christians from ever again committing sin. Christians are not the poster children for moral excellence nor should we attempt to represent ourselves as such. When the perpetrators of this misrepresentation are questioned concerning whether or not they themselves are perfect, they cunningly respond that they are guilty only of sinning by default, or unknowingly. If you choose to categorize sin as small, insignificant, cardinal, deliberate, or un-deliberate, it is your prerogative- but do not expect God to; sin is sin. Make no mistake about it, sin separates from God, and always leads to death. If we are going to be with God in eternity we must become saved through the blood of Jesus. Morality is surely a desired outcome, but it is not a condition for salvation.

This does not reduce the need of a person to adhere to the tenets of morality, as these events will certainly rate high on the believer's Day of

Judgment.[45] Our regular attendance to the study of God's word lends the strength that gives us the ability to press that proverbial five hundred pound weight. The more we study, pray, and worship God, the stronger we become. With our spiritually enhanced strength we are able to minimize the crushing power of the weight of sin. Disobedience to God will render us weak and certainly subject even to death in the flesh. The Spirit of God leads a believer from within and not from without. The latter represents the Old Testament where God's people were guided and judged by the law. Conversely, the New Testament established that after Jesus, His followers would be led by the Holy Spirit indwelled within each member. The one and most important difference is that in order to be a Christian, you must be **BORN AGAIN**. So again: Salvation is becoming something, not doing something.

What have we learned of our salvation? That Jesus Christ is the manifestation of God on earth to redeem His creation.[46] The law, as a mirror, reflects our true being which is unfit for relationship with God.[47] Having acknowledged this in repentance, we ask God for forgiveness. Our asking is a product of conversion where we surrender self with the full understanding that we have asked God to enter our souls and take command of our ultimate will. When you surrender to God through the acceptance of Him in the manifestation of human sacrifice, "Jesus the Christ", God regenerates you, and you are saved.[48] Having become a new creature, you are assured of your destiny and the abolition of the penalty of sin, "eternal damnation".[49] The power of sin, "death" will plague you until you are free from the presence of sin, lust. Paul assured the believers in Corinth that nothing would befall them that God had not given them the power to overcome:

> *There hath no temptation taken you but such as is common to man: but God is faithful, who will not suffer you to be tempted*

---

45 Romans 6:15 What then? shall we sin, because we are not under the law, but under grace? God forbid.
46 Isaiah 44:24 Thus saith the LORD, thy redeemer, and he that formed thee from the womb, I am the LORD that maketh all things; that stretcheth forth the heavens alone; that spreadeth abroad the earth by myself;
47 Romans 7:5 For when we were in the flesh, the motions of sins, which were by the law, did work in our members to bring forth fruit unto death.
48 Romans 10:9 That if thou shalt confess with thy mouth the Lord Jesus, and shalt believe in thine heart that God hath raised him from the dead, thou shalt be saved.
49 Romans 8:1 There is therefore now no condemnation to them which are in Christ Jesus, who walk not after the flesh, but after the Spirit.

above that ye are able; but will with the temptation also make a way to escape, that ye may be able to bear it.

1 Corinthians 10:13

We Need Jesus!

In the final analysis, salvation is not a badge, it is a reality. It is not based on something that you did; it is something that only God can do. You do not have the power to create it and therefore you do not have the power to destroy it. In as much as you didn't find it you are incapable of losing it.[50] When you figure out how to give your physical existence back to your earthly parents, you will have figured out how to give your spiritual existence back to your heavenly father. Having received it, you are to become obedient to the indwelling Spirit that leads you.[51] While disobedience to its direction may cost you your physical life, your spiritual life is secured forever in Christ.[52]

If you don't read another page in this book, please know that Jesus loves you so much, that He died for you.[53] He is knocking on your heart and begging you to let Him come in.[54] He wants to wash you with His blood, and present you faultless before His throne.[55] Acknowledge your sins by repenting, and allow Him in by simply asking Him to save you.[56] Having faith in His ability is the only work that you need to do to be saved.[57] Jesus' death is His payment for your sins, which relieves you of the debt by mercy

---

[50] John 15:16 Ye have not chosen me, but I have chosen you, and ordained you, that ye should go and bring forth fruit, and that your fruit should remain: that whatsoever ye shall ask of the Father in my name, he may give it you.

[51] Hebrews 6:1

[52] Romans 6:12 Let not sin therefore reign in your mortal body, that ye should obey it in the lusts thereof.

[53] John 3:16 For God so loved the world, that he gave his only begotten Son, that whosoever believeth in him should not perish, but have everlasting life.

[54] Revelation 3:20 Behold, I stand at the door, and knock: if any man hear my voice, and open the door, I will come in to him, and will sup with him, and he with me.

[55] Jude 1:24 Now unto him that is able to keep you from falling, and to present you faultless before the presence of his glory with exceeding joy,

[56] Matthew 7:7 Ask, and it shall be given you; seek, and ye shall find; knock, and it shall be opened unto you:

[57] 2 Timothy 1:9 Who hath saved us, and called us with an holy calling, not according to our works, but according to his own purpose and grace, which was given us in Christ Jesus before the world began,

and gives you eternal life by grace. You are then justified i.e. "saved".⁵⁸ Call on Him right now; pray and ask Him to enter your heart. Let your whole being be permeated with His spiritual presence⁵⁹ and you are saved.⁶⁰

---

58 Acts 13:39 And by him all that believe are justified from all things, from which ye could not be justified by the law of Moses.
59 Romans 12:1 I beseech you therefore, brethren, by the mercies of God, that ye present your bodies a living sacrifice, holy, acceptable unto God, which is your reasonable service.
60 Romans 10:10-13 For with the heart man believeth unto righteousness; and with the mouth confession is made unto salvation. For the scripture saith, Whosoever believeth on him shall not be ashamed. For there is no difference between the Jew and the Greek: for the same Lord over all is rich unto all that call upon him. For whosoever shall call upon the name of the Lord shall be saved.

CHURCH ORDINANCES

The family of God receives instructions through Church ordinances that distinguish them from the family of the world. In Greek, the term ordinance denotes a "dogma," a law, or decree thus, it presupposes an authority or government. Church ordinances are very useful in defining the key elements of a Christian establishment's bible interpretation. They represent the authority of that Church as well as how its members are disciplined.[61] Ordinances vary between different Churches and or denominations. These differences are a matter of interpretation of the scriptures by the authority of the Church. In some Church circles there are two ordinances: Baptism and Communion. In others there are three or more.

The scriptures establish two ordinances that reveal what would otherwise be invisible. We shall examine these ordinances relative to their meaning and purpose. We will also consider one ordinance that some Churches believe to be a requirement yet I will demonstrate is not.

As we have implied, the Church is an orderly body of believers under the direction of Christ Jesus. We often talk of joining the Church as though it is a club or social organization. Unfortunately, many Churches have allowed themselves to digress to this description. Peter taught that the Lord added to the Church daily such as should be saved.[62] So, the Church is a living organism, the bride of Christ Jesus.

Jesus' love for the Church is represented by His sacrificial death. Our

---

61 Romans 13:2 Whosoever therefore resisteth the power, resisteth the ordinance of God: and they that resist shall receive to themselves damnation.
62 Acts 2:47 Praising God, and having favour with all the people. And the Lord added to the Church daily such as should be saved.

love for Jesus should be represented by our submission to His will.[63] When we proclaim Jesus as our Lord we surrender our will to Him. The baptism and communion are both meant to be witnessed by the Church as acts of submission to the expressed will of the Father. Let us now examine both of these ordinances.

Baptism is the ordinance that represents our relationship with God, whereas the Communion is the ordinance that represents our fellowship. Since we must have a relationship before fellowship we will consider these ordinances in that order.

---

63 Revelation 2:10 Fear none of those things which thou shalt suffer: behold, the devil shall cast some of you into prison, that ye may be tried; and ye shall have tribulation ten days: be thou faithful unto death, and I will give thee a crown of life.

BAPTISM

Baptism is important as it symbolizes the reality of our new birth, and our obedience to the instructions of the Lord. Through baptism we identify with the unique family of Christ, "The Church."

1. What constitutes Baptism?
2. What precedes Baptism?
3. What does Baptism symbolize?

What Constitutes Baptism?

The Greek word Baptizo means to dip, immerse or submerge. In other words, "baptize" refers to something being buried.[64] The early Church buried members in water to satisfy this ordinance. As time progressed however, the Church began substituting baptism by submergence with sprinkling or pouring to accommodate the sick and bed-ridden. After a while, many Churches ceased adhering to the ordinance of submerging altogether; preferring the less cumbersome and least expensive methods. According to the Scriptures, Jesus went down into the water, and subsequently came up out of the water.[65] Sprinkling or pouring would not have required His bodily presence in the water. Adhering to the ordinance of baptism necessitates full submersion just as our Lord Jesus demonstrated.

This ordinance is to be administered during a regular worship service and not at home or some private place. Those who opt to obscure locations

---

64 Colossians 2:12 Buried with him in baptism, wherein also ye are risen with him through the faith of the operation of God, who hath raised him from the dead.
65 Matthew 3:16

for the baptism are usually doing so because of the fear of not being accepted by Jesus until the act of baptism is fulfilled. As we will discuss next, baptism itself does nothing to enhance the believers' salvation.

Jesus instructed His disciples not to be ashamed of Him or to fear the inevitable persecutions that were to occur. [66] Baptism is the believers' testimony to the world that without a doubt, Jesus the Christ is God.[67] The saints who publicly acknowledged Jesus and His works during the days of Christ's ministry were often persecuted.[68]

What Precedes Baptism?

The second factor relates to that which should precede Baptism. Baptism is the believer's testimony of faith to the Church.[69] It should not be viewed as synonymous with regeneration. Reverend Dr. Cyrus A. Weaver, the beloved deceased pastor of Day Springs Baptist Church in Jacksonville, Florida, said on one occasion, "If baptism could save you, I would go to the zoo and baptize every monkey I see." This wise pastor was not speaking of the salvation of monkeys, he was relating to the fact that baptism does not save. Just as the thief on the cross was saved yet not baptized, it is reiterated that water baptism is not a requirement for salvation.[70]

What is required for salvation however is regeneration (being born again). Regeneration is the *scriptural* prerequisite for baptism but, it also has prerequisites of its own. Before regeneration can occur, a person must both repent and be converted/convinced. Conversion is the surrender of man's will unto God's. So the sequence for baptism is:

Repentance/Conversion → Regeneration → Baptism

Maybe you were baptized as a requirement for joining a Church; however

---

66 Luke 9:26 Matthew 10:28
67 John 20:28
68 Matthew 10:28 And fear not them which kill the body, but are not able to kill the soul: but rather fear him which is able to destroy both soul and body in hell.
69 Acts 8:36-37 And as they went on their way, they came unto a certain water: and the eunuch said, See, here is water; what doth hinder me to be baptized? And Philip said, If thou believest with all thine heart, thou mayest. And he answered and said, I believe that Jesus Christ is the Son of God.
70 Luke 23:43

joining a Church is not equivalent to being saved and one should not be baptized for admission into a Church unless joining is a confession to being saved. Baptism relates to the believer's position in Christ so if one submits to baptism without having been born again, the baptism is unscriptural and therefore has no spiritual meaning.[71]

Baptism Symbolizes What?

The third factor deals with symbolism. "A symbol is something that represents something else by association, resemblance, or convention, especially a material object used to represent something invisible."[72] It stands to reason that baptism must symbolize being saved, since being saved must precede it. In line with the definition of a "symbol", we represent the need to be saved and the objects are the believer and the water. We are all born in sin. The Bible says there is none righteous no not one.[73] The wages of sin is death.[74] We are to symbolize that very death in a testimony, verbal and otherwise. Christ confirmed this when He commanded that we be baptized.[75]

The first step is to submit to that which symbolizes your faith. Paul gave a discourse to this symbolism in the 6th chapter of Romans. Through baptism, we are buried with Him, made dead to the world, and raised to life. Think of it, you stand in the water, with the water level crossing your body.

a. Your body is the vertical plain and the water is the horizontal. Can you see the cross?
   i. This symbolizes Christ's death for sin,
   ii. your death to sin, and
   iii. your future death to this sinful world.

b. You are submerged in the water.
   i. This symbolizes Christ's burial,
   ii. the burial of the old you, and
   iii. your future separation from the flesh.

---

71 Because the baptism is an outward confession of having already been saved, children under the age of accountability are exempt from this ordinance. (See Acts 10:47)
72 Collins English Dictionary
73 Romans 3:10
74 Romans 6:23
75 Matthew 28:19

   c. You are brought up out of the water.
- i. This symbolizes the resurrection of Christ,
- ii. your new life, and
- iii. the final victory of death and the grave.[76]

How can so much be symbolized by sprinkling and pouring?

Jesus told Nicodemus that one had to be born of the water (flesh birth) and of the Spirit (spiritual birth) so we *represent* this process with a physical demonstration of a spiritual realization. Going down into the baptismal waters represents death, just as in the days of Noah (the flood), and emerging out of the water represents life, as in the spiritual birth (being born again). Some would like to associate water with the fact that the saints of God are "washed" from their sins. Although the bible speaks of being washed with pure water, salvation certainly cannot be attained in a baptism pool.[77] Our washing comes from the actual blood of Jesus, which paid the ransom for our sins.

> *But one of the soldiers with a spear pierced his side, and forthwith came there out <u>blood and water</u>.*   John 19:34

> *And from Jesus Christ, who is the faithful witness, and the first begotten of the dead, and the prince of the kings of the earth. Unto him that loved us, and <u>washed us from our sins in his own blood,</u>*   Revelation 1:5

> *And I said unto him, Sir, thou knows. And he said to me, These are they which came out of great tribulation, and have <u>washed their robes, and made them white in the blood of the Lamb.</u>*   Revelation 7:14

The above scriptures reveal a deliverance from death. The baptism is a public testimony of a believer's confession that Jesus Christ has, through

---

76 1 Corinthians 15:54 So when this corruptible shall have put on incorruption, and this mortal shall have put on immortality, then shall be brought to pass the saying that is written, Death is swallowed up in victory.

77 Hebrews 10:22 Let us draw near with a true heart in full assurance of faith, having our hearts sprinkled from an evil conscience, and our bodies washed with pure water.

the Holy Spirit, entered their souls and rendered them a new creature. We came from our mother's womb by way of water, this was the beginning of our earthily life. Just as our earthily life began by birth, our spiritual life also begins by birth, spiritual birth. Spiritual birth is invisible and personal; therefore the world is given notice of this occasion by the submission of the new convert to the ordinance of baptism.[78]

In whose name?

Now we will investigate the issue of *in whose name* the ordinance is to be administered. Some Church administrations baptize their members strictly "in the name of Jesus Christ."[79] They do so in harmony with the circumstances at Pentecost, where after hearing Peter preach the Gospel, those who gladly received His word were baptized; and the same day there was added unto them about three thousand souls.[80] Here, we can see the process of salvation. It was said of Jesus:

> *But as many as received him, to them gave he power to become the sons of God, even to them that believe on his name:*
> John 1:12

Note the following question and answer:

Question:

> *Now when they heard this, they were pricked in their heart, and said unto Peter and to the rest of the apostles, Men and brethren, <u>what shall we do?</u>*
> Acts 2:37

Answer:

> *"Repent, and be baptized <u>every one of you in the name of Jesus Christ</u> for the remission of sins, <u>and ye shall</u> receive the gift of the Holy Ghost."*
> Acts 2:38

---

78 John 3:6 That which is born of the flesh is flesh; and that which is born of the Spirit is spirit.
79 Acts 2:38
80 Acts 2:41

According to *Matthew 28:19* however, the baptism ordinance is to be administered in the name of the Father, the Son, and the Holy Ghost. So the question now becomes, "which is appropriate: baptizing in the name of Jesus Christ or in the name of the Father, the Son, and the Holy Ghost?"

Christ came to save all sorts of people. His instruction to the disciples was that they go and teach all nations. Since Jesus commissioned His disciples to teach all men, the entire world became their mission field.[81] Those who were not born into the family of God could now become sons of God. Keep in mind though, that the Jews had not yet converted and accepted Jesus as the Christ so the disciples began preaching first in regions occupied by Israel.[82]

As noted above in Acts chapter two, the commission being administered by Peter at Pentecost was given exclusively to the House of Israel.[83] What distinguished the House of Israel from all others was their prior acknowledgement of Jehovah and His personal acknowledgement of them. No other nation had the benefit of such a relationship with God. Since Israel was already closely acquainted with God the Father and God the Holy Ghost, they were separated only by their denial of Jesus Christ as Lord (before anyone can be born again they must receive Jesus as God). Due to their unique circumstance, Jews needed only to be baptized in the name of Jesus. Not so for the rest of us.

Also note that prior to Jesus' departure; no natural Jew was ever required to submit to baptism; only proselytes converting *to* the Jewish faith needed to be baptized. Now the Jewish alter of repentance had become the public baptism site. This public baptism served as the Jewish convert's testimony acknowledging Christ as God.[84] Such was the only missing component for a believer of the House of Israel.

Further proof that Peter's directions in Acts chapter two applied solely to Israelites and not Gentiles (those not of the Jewish faith) is seen in the fact

---

81 Matthew 28:19
82 Acts 1:8 But ye shall receive power, after that the Holy Ghost is come upon you: and ye shall be witnesses unto me both in Jerusalem, and in all Judaea, and in Samaria, and unto the uttermost part of the earth.
83 Acts 2:36 Therefore let all the house of Israel know assuredly, that God hath made that same Jesus, whom ye have crucified, both Lord and Christ.
84 Acts 2:37-38 Now when they heard this, they were pricked in their heart, and said unto Peter and to the rest of the apostles, Men and brethren, what shall we do? Then Peter said unto them, Repent, and be baptized every one of you in the name of Jesus Christ for the remission of sins, and ye shall receive the gift of the Holy Ghost.

that Peter did not associate with Gentiles until after his roof top experience in Acts 10:9-16. Only after his divinely arranged meeting with Cornelius did Peter began professing that God was no respecter of persons.[85] Also note that the gentiles received their salvation prior to being baptized which differed from the orthodox Jew.[86]

Is Salvation in The Name?

When we say, "in the name of," we mean, "in the power of." Our claim of eternal salvation must encompass our past, present and future. This is satisfied in the God-Head since the Father assures the present, the Son covers our past, and the Holy Ghost secures our future. The appropriate baptism must symbolize that which was, is, and is to come. When you attempt to isolate the personage of God you rob yourself of the full understanding associated with His revelation. A Jew standing in the baptismal pool represents one who has the presence of God as a nation, the Promise of God as their hope and the Person of God as their salvation. Contrast this with a Gentile standing in the pool without instruction, conversion, nor regeneration and you have nothing symbolizing the presence, promise or person of God. Gentiles must acknowledge God through learning, repentance, conversion, and regeneration.

Peter addressed baptism as it related to John the Baptist's teachings.

> *That word, I say, ye know, which was published throughout all Judaea, and began from Galilee, after the baptism which John preached; How <u>God</u> anointed <u>Jesus</u> of Nazareth with the <u>Holy Ghost</u> and with power: who went about doing good, and healing all that were oppressed of the devil; for God was with him.*
>
> Acts 10:37-38

Peter was teaching relative to the *Father, Son* and *Holy Ghost*. This was necessary since the Gentile brethren were not governed by either personification of the Godhead. Peter expounded on how God anointed Jesus of Nazareth with the Holy Ghost and with power. At the conclusion,

---

85 Acts 10:34
86 Acts 10:47 Can any man forbid water, that these should not be baptized, which have received the Holy Ghost as well as we?

hat they be baptized in the name of the Lord. Some bible ... the word "Lord" to "Jesus" here. While Jesus certainly ... in this case is material since Peter was here giving ... Gentiles who needed to be baptized in the name of all three ...ges unlike the Jews, who needed to be baptized in the name of Jesus only.[87] Peter knew all too well that the power of the baptism lie in the name of the Lord/Jesus, God/Father, and the Almighty/Holy Ghost.

Revelation 1:8 records God's name as: *"I Am Alpha and Omega"* and describes Him as that *"which is, and which was, and which is to come, the Almighty."* Hence our baptism symbolizes that our past, present and future are secure.[88] The term Almighty signifies omnipotence and transcends the existence of competing authority.[89] To deny this scriptural fact is to put to shame the work of Jesus Christ in salvation. Therefore we appropriately entreat:

> ➤ "In the Name of the "Father *"which is*(Give us this day) and
> ➤ "In the Name of the "Son *"which was* (Forgive our debts) and
> ➤ "In the Name of the "Holy Ghost *"which is to come* (Lead us not into temptation).[90]

Consider the following scriptures:

> *Behold, he cometh with clouds; and every eye shall see him, and they also which pierced him: and all kindreds of the earth shall wail because of him. Even so, Amen.* **I am Alpha and Omega, the beginning and the ending, saith the Lord, which is, and which was, and which is to come, the Almighty.**
> Revelation 1:7-8

> *Hearken unto me, O Jacob and Israel, my called;* **I am he; I am the first, I also am the last.** Isaiah 48:12

In Isaiah, the scripture represents Jehovah as Alpha and Omega. In

---

87 Rev 1:8, 4:8, 11:17, 15:3, 16:7, 16:14, and 21: 22
88 Revelation 4:8"...Lord God Almighty, which was, and is, and is to come."
89 Matthew 28:18 And Jesus came and spake unto them, saying, All power is given unto me in heaven and in earth.
90 Colossians 1:4, 5

Revelation, the scripture is representing Jesus as Alpha and Omega. The redemption qualities of God are only realized in His human form.[91] He was pierced by man, and had also been kindred of man; this refers to His redeeming qualities.[92] The kinsman redeemer needed to be a member of the human family. At the same time, He is eternal; as indicated by the designation "Alpha and Omega".

When we speak of God in a language that makes Him discernible, we naturally and automatically associate Him with something visible although He is invisible. The following Scripture points our minds to the very physical appearance of God the Father.[93]

> *And I heard a great voice out of heaven saying, Behold,* **the tabernacle of God is with men,** *and he will dwell with them, and they shall be his people, and* **God himself shall be with them, and be their God.** *And* **God shall wipe away all tears from their eyes;** *and there shall be no more death, neither sorrow, nor crying, neither shall there be any more pain: for the former things are passed away. And he that sat upon the throne said, Behold, I make all things new. And* **he said unto me,** *Write: for these words are true and faithful. And he said unto me, It is done.* **I am Alpha and Omega,** *the beginning and the end. I will give unto him that is athirst of the fountain of the water of life freely. He that overcometh shall inherit all things; and* <u>**I will be his God**</u>, *and he shall be my son.*
>
> Revelation 21:3-7

If you go back and read only the bold print of the preceding scripture you will not be able to deny that God is referencing Himself as physically coming to be with His people. In the first chapter of Revelation the Alpha and Omega was Jesus. In the twenty-first chapter the Alpha and Omega is God. Without a doubt there can be but one beginning and but one ending. The Bible does not distinguish between the person of God the Father and

---

91 Philippians 2:6 Who, being in the form of God, thought it not robbery to be equal with God:
92 Acts 20:28 Take heed therefore unto yourselves, and to all the flock, over the which the Holy Ghost hath made you overseers, to feed the Church of God, which he hath purchased with his own blood.
93 1 Timothy 6:16

God the Son, unless it is giving us a perspective from which we can interpret the otherwise incomprehensible presence of God.[94]

As you are born once, you are re-born only once and therefore should not be baptized but once in your Christian walk. Remember, a scriptural baptism, by necessity, occurs *after* your spiritual re-birth.

*"**One Lord, one faith, one baptism,**"*
Ephesians 4:5

---

[94] Malachi 2:10, Mark 12:32, Romans 3:30, 1Corinthians 8:6, Ephesians 4:6, 1Timothy 2:5, and James 2:19.

COMMUNION
The Lord's Supper

The term Communion is derived from the Latin word communio (sharing in common). The corresponding term in Greek is κοινωνία, and is often translated as "fellowship". Communion is something that we *"do in remembrance"* of Jesus.[95] It is our means of publicly and collectively acknowledging the reality that the Lord is in us, and that we are in Him. It is a highly symbolic commemoration in that it represents a multitude of spiritual truths. It is the ordinance that symbolizes our fellowship and relationship with God and our personal commitment to work out His will. The communion also represents our association and service in the House of the Lord. More importantly, the communion is a memorial representing the reality that we are new spirit creatures, indwelled by the Holy Spirit, requiring spiritual food by which we grow based on consumption. Being born again renders us hungry for the Word of God.[96] We are new creatures, spiritually reborn, so our food must be spiritually received. We begin with milk and progress to strong meat. This is symbolic of our growing to spiritual maturity through the Holy Spirit. Jesus said unto them,

> *"Verily, verily I say unto you. Except ye eat the flesh of the Son of man, and drink His blood, ye have no life in you,"*
> John 6:53

Jesus went on to explain to His disciples what it meant for them to

---

95 1Corinthians 11:24
96 1 Peter 2:2 As newborn babes, desire the sincere milk of the word, that ye may grow thereby:

consume Him. This concept was very difficult for the disciples to understand. Jesus replied:

> *"the words I speak unto you, they are spirit, and they are life."*
> John 6:63

The key word in the Communion is "remembrance". We are to remember the Lord's sufferings, death, and especially His resurrection, through which we have been granted the gift of eternal life. It consists of bread, representing Christ's suffering, and of wine, which represents His blood poured out for the remission of our sins. It is symbolic of the walk *with* Christ that follows the birth *in* Christ, which was symbolized by baptism. The memorial of the Last Supper is of special importance to the believer for all these reasons but primarily because we are commanded by the Lord Himself to memorialize the dinner that He effectually modeled during the Last Supper with the disciples.

> *"And He took the cup, and gave thanks, and said, Take this, and divide it among yourselves: For I say unto you, I will not drink of the fruit of the vine, until the Kingdom of God shall come. And He took bread, and gave thanks, and brake it, and gave unto them, saying, this is my body which is given for you: this do in remembrance of me,"*
> Luke 22:17-19

The frequency is indicated in these words,

> *"...as oft as ye drink it, in remembrance of me,"*
> I Corinthians 11:25

"As oft" means, as determined by you. In this case, the "you," is the Church. As a ritual, we are to formally memorialize Christ as often as we choose to do so.

The assurance of our fellowship rests solely on our faith in Christ Jesus. John gave us the Lord's condition for such assurance.

> *"If we confess our sins, he is faithful and just to forgive us our sins, and to cleanse us from all unrighteousness."*
> I John 1:9

The Greek word for confess is homologeō. It is composed of two words; *homo* which means "together with or as same" and *logos*, which means "thoughtful word, to speak to confess, i.e. to admit or declare one's self guilty of what one is accused of". Therefore, the word *confess* means "to speak word as same or agree". The Lord teaches us to agree with Him concerning our fellowship and that He will forgive any and all sins. Such agreement is a product of our personal acknowledgement of the Spirit of God speaking in our lives.

Remember that although you are born again and no longer subject to the penalty of sin (eternal damnation), you are not immune to the consequences brought on by satanic lusts, which can led to physical death. Communion therefore, represents our need to be open and responsive to the very presence of the Holy Spirit as He guides us through our walk with Christ. The Lord's Supper, Communion, is the public demonstration of the memorial of Christ.[97]

---

97 I John 1:9

SUBSTANTIATIONS

Substantiation is the doctrine of the literal changing of the substance used in the Communion from a material purpose to a spiritual purpose. The more popular interpretations of these are relative to the doctrines of the Catholic faith (Transubstantiation), the Lutheran faith (Consubstantiation), and the Episcopalian faith (the receiving of favor from God). We will conclude with the Congregationalist view (a memorial). The first two, trans & consubstantiation, are considered to be miracle transformations rendering the actual body of Jesus to coexist in the latter or exist in the former ritual.

TRANSUBSTANTIATION

The first, transubstantiation, means to change or transfer one substance into another. "In Roman Catholic theology, transubstantiation means the change, in the Eucharist, of the substance of wheat bread and grape wine into the substance of the Body and the Blood of Jesus, while all that is accessible to the senses (the appearances - species in Latin) remains as before. In the case of the Eucharist of the Catholic Church, the bread and wine are changed into the actual body of Christ."[98]

CONSUBSTANTIATION

"Consubstantiation is a theological doctrine that (like Transubstantiation) attempts to describe the nature of the Christian Eucharist in concrete metaphysical terms. It holds that during the sacrament, the fundamental

---

98 From Wikipedia, the free encyclopedia

"substance" of the body and blood of Christ are present alongside the substance of the bread and wine, which remain present."[99]

EPISCOPAL

The Episcopalians say that it is not a matter of the actual body or blood, but, the receiving of more favor with God through the partaking of Communion. "In the Eucharist or Holy Communion service, the Book of Common Prayer specifies that bread and wine are consecrated for consumption by the people. Those wishing for whatever reason to avoid alcohol are free to decline the cup. A Eucharist can be part of a wedding to celebrate a sacramental marriage and of a funeral as a thank offering (sacrifice) to God and for the comfort of the mourners."[100]

MEMORIAL

Churches believing in merely the symbolism of the bread and wine agree with Ulrich Zwingli[101] that the physical body is not in the bread or the wine. The communion is the memorial service of Christ.

The communion is administered in one of three methods; closed, close, or open. The *closed* communion is one that refuses the right of communion to outsiders who are not identified as members of their unique fellowship. The *close* communion requires the Church to provide instructions prior to the actual consumption. In contrast, all who come to an *open* communion may participate without examination or consideration of fellowship with the Church.

First Corinthians chapter eleven establishes the appropriate stipulations for administering the "Lord's Supper." Only those who are able to discern[102] His body are welcomed. Anyone else *"eateth and drinketh damnation to himself"*. This means that only the saved and committed are in fellowship and should join in the feast. While there is no magic involved in the consumption of the bread and wine, you are reminded that doing so is publicly announcing that

---

99 From Wikipedia, the free encyclopedia
100 From Wikipedia, the free encyclopedia
101 Ulrich Zwingli (1484-1531) was a Swiss theologian who was an early leader in the Protestant Reformation and who helped created one of the main branches of Protestantism, known as the Reformed Tradition.
102 To perceive or recognize as being different or distinct; distinguish.

Jesus is the head of your life and that you are in continuous communication with Him. Paul cautioned the saints that to take part in this communion inappropriately was to invite serious or even deadly consequences into one's life. For this reason, the minister should lead by instructing his congregation on the criteria for partaking. This is an example of a "Close Communion."

RITUALIZATION VS. REALIZATION

Rituals in the form of religion have been used to control the masses since the days of Noah, Ham, Cush and Nimrod. A quick look back at the inaugural po-ligious (Political/Religious) institutions reveal similar teachings of many of the miraculous events associated with the Communion. Jesus' purpose on earth brought spiritual liberty to all who would receive Him. However, many of those who witnessed His great powers were only interested in His earthily potential. As John reflected in the sixth chapter of his Gospel, Jesus, after feeding the people, had to retreat from them as they were pursuing Him *"to make him a king,"*.[103] They were apparently motivated by the fact that He had miraculously fed so many of them. Jesus did what no other human being could do; He took very little and fed many. Jesus was demonstrating to the masses His ability to provide. The political purpose of religious control was seen in the response of those who followed Jesus, *"What shall we do, that we might work the works of God?"* Jesus responded, *"This is the work of God,* **that you believe on him whom he hath sent.**"[104] Certainly, *"him whom he hath sent"* is none other than Jesus. Believing that men and or institutions have the power to randomly perform miracles is synonymous with agreeing that men can *"work the works of God"*. No, we cannot change the bread or the wine; we may only thankfully receive it in commemoration of *"the works of God"* through our Lord Jesus Christ.

Some churches discourage participation by those who have not been physically baptized. One problem with such interference is that it most often discourages a church's recent members who perhaps, have not yet had the opportunity to be baptized. Typically, before a person is admitted into

---

103 John 6:14, 15
104 John 6:28, 29

a Church as an official "member", he or she is questioned for the purpose of determining salvation. Upon such affirmative determination, the privileges of fellowship should be gained based on the believer's relationship with Christ. To then deny a member communion because they have not been physically baptized is synonymous with saying, "you aren't really saved until you complete the first ordinance". How many Churches are guilty of such practices yet allow strangers of whom they have no knowledge of to take part? The truth of the matter is simply this; those you think are worthy might not be, and vice versa. While baptism is indeed a commandment, it is not a prerequisite of salvation. It is no wonder that the Apostle Paul instructed the Church at Corinth to examine themselves:

> *But let a man examine himself, and so let him eat of that bread, and drink of that cup. For he that eateth and drinketh unworthily, eateth and drinketh damnation to himself, not discerning the Lord's body. For this cause many are weak and sickly among you, and many sleep. For if we would judge ourselves, we should not be judged.*   1 Corinthians 11:28-31

Washing Feet

At the Last Supper, Jesus witnessed His disciples quarreling over who was greatest. He then insisted on washing the disciples' feet.[105] He did this to demonstrate the duty of a servant. Peter desperately resisted the notion. Jesus then vowed that if Peter did not allow Him to wash his feet that Peter would not be with Him in heaven.[106] Peter agreed to not only his feet, but also his hands and his head.

As a result, some congregations have added the doctrine of feet washing to the list of recognized and required ordinances. This interpretation omits the greater inference of what it means to be a servant. Keep in mind that ordinances are symbolic, physical expressions of spiritual truths that cannot be detected by the human eye. Being saved is not something that you can see; therefore baptism serves as the physical representation of this spiritual, invisible event. Likewise, we demonstrate our fellowship with God with the

---

105 John 13:5 After that he poureth water into a bason, and began to wash the disciples' feet, and to wipe them with the towel wherewith he was girded.
106 John 13:8

communion. Both are invisible occurrences requiring visible representation. Feet washing, however, is a physical event used as an example to illustrate another physical event. The service that Jesus was modeling for the disciples was not invisible; Jesus was showing His disciples that service is literal. The disciples needed to understand their role as servants. Christ was emphasizing that His followers were to be of humble dispositions as they serve mankind. The proper way to submit to this command is through actual service; not rituals. The washing of feet is not something that should be symbolized; it is something that should be actualized.[107]

> *If I then, your Lord and Master, have washed your feet; ye also ought to wash one another's feet. For I have given you an example, that ye should do as I have done to you. Verily, verily, I say unto you, The servant is not greater than his lord; neither he that is sent greater than he that sent him. If ye know these things, happy are ye if ye do them.* John 13:14-17

> *Let not a widow be taken into the number under threescore years old, having been the wife of one man. Well reported of for good works; if she have brought up children, if she have lodged strangers, **if she have washed the saints' feet**, if she have relieved the afflicted, if she have diligently followed every good work.*
> 1Timothy 5:9, 10

The woman referenced by Timothy was a servant of the church and was noted for the appropriate execution of God's commands. She washed feet as a service rather than a ritual. If we are to accept the washing of feet as an ordinance, then we should also consider the bringing up of children, the lodging of strangers, and relieving the afflicted as the same. Conversely, the example set forth here reveals the path that every believer should follow daily and not on occasion. Jesus said of Himself,

> *"Even as the Son of man came not to be ministered unto, but to minister, and to give his life a ransom for many."*
> Matthew 20:28

---

[107] 1 Timothy 5:10 Washed the Saints feet

In the final analysis, the Communion represents the spiritual reality of our Lord and Saviour existing within our souls. We honor His presence through the memorial service that reveals this truth. There are no hooks, or special miracles outside of the miracle of the New Birth which is represented by you, "The Saved".

STEWARDSHIP

A steward, by definition, is "one who manages another's property, finances, or other affairs; an administrator; supervisor". On the sixth day of creation, light, water and land had already been organized by God. The world was populated with every inhabitant for the exception of man.

> *"And God said, let us make man in our image, after our likeness: and let them have dominion over the fish of the sea, and over the cattle, and over all the earth, and over every creeping thing that creepeth upon the earth.*   Genesis 1:26

Upon the Lord's command to *"let them have dominion . . ."* man was appointed steward of the entire world and given the privilege and responsibility of overseeing the earth according to God's instructions. Herein begins the line which distinguishes the Master from the steward. The acknowledgment of stewardship by the steward must be accompanied by obedience to the master. In the case of humanity, this acknowledgement and obedience is directly proportionate to our fellowship with God.

I like to think of management as the ability to *do things right* and leadership as the ability to *do the right thing*. The manager must have a clear and defined set of procedures to follow. The leader will often change and establish procedures as he goes. In the capacity of stewards, we are managers. We have a clear and concise set of rules and principles that we adhere to. The Bible contains the divine principles by which all human conduct, creeds, and opinions shall be tried. Therefore, when you consider this world and its contents, ask yourself the following questions:

1. What does God Own?

2. What do you own?
3. What do you control?

Don't you think that it is clear, considering the Word of God, that He created everything visible and invisible, and that He created them for Himself?

> *For by him were all things created, that are in heaven, and that are in earth, visible and invisible, whether they be thrones, or dominions, or principalities, or powers: all things were created by him, and for him: And he is before all things, and by him all things consist. And he is the head of the body, the Church: who is the beginning, the firstborn from the dead; that in all things he might have the preeminence.*   Colossians 1:16-18

From this alone, it is clear to see that God owns everything. That God owns everything presupposes that we own nothing. However; when we consider what God owns, we must also consider what He has made us responsible for.

> *And God said, Let us make man in our image, after our likeness: and let them have dominion over the fish of the sea, and over the fowl of the air, and over the cattle, and over all the earth, and over every creeping thing that creepeth upon the earth. So God created man in his own image, in the image of God created he him; male and female created he them. And God blessed them, and God said unto them, Be fruitful, and multiply, and replenish the earth, and subdue it: and have dominion over the fish of the sea, and over the fowl of the air, and over every living thing that moveth upon the earth.*   Genesis 1:26-28

There is an International Youth Group called Jesus Cadets International," who has as its Outdoor Code:

> *As a human being, I do my best to*
> *Be considerate of my environment*
> *Be responsible for stewardship*
> *Be a protector of innocent creatures*
> *Be thankful for God's blessings*

These youth are being taught at a very young and impressionable age the importance of stewardship. We are caretakers of the earth. We do not own the earth nor will we ever. The earth is the Lord's and the fullness thereof.[108]

Remember that managers do things right and leaders do the right thing. In all things, there is need for training and study in order to function in accordance with the design and purpose. Managing God's earthly creation is humanity's purpose. When you think of judgment you should consider whether or not you have been acceptably accountable for the things that God has placed in your care.

> *"Who then is that faithful Steward, whom his Lord shall make ruler over his household, to give them their portion of meat in due season? Blessed is that servant, whom his Lord when he cometh shall find so doing. Of a truth I say unto you, that he will make him ruler over all that he hath.* Luke 12:42-44

In our last lesson, we discussed the ordinances of the Church. We acknowledged them as authoritative commands. Complying with the instructions concerning the ordinances is the new believer's first act of obedience. The next step is expanding the responsibilities of fellowship into every walk of our lives.

Stewardship deals with the experiential sanctification[109] phase of a believer's life. It is the measuring rod of a believer's growth and development in the Holy Spirit. Remember Peter initially understood leadership as being a position of status and therefore resisted the Lord's attempt to wash his feet. He was made to understand that the greatest among us must become the servant to us all. Selfishness and personal bias cause us to desire things that are pleasing to us, rather than to God. However, as stewards, we are now under a higher authority. The blessed fact that our bodies are the temple of The Holy Spirit has two sides; that He is ours and we are His. The believer was purchased on Golgotha's Hill.[110] The price paid was the blood of

---

108 1 Corinthians 10:26
109 Experiential sanctification is the evidence of the Power of God in our lives. (Born Again)
110 The place where Jesus was crucified. "Calvary"

God's only begotten Son.[111] This has profound significance for the believer. The significance is that we do not belong to ourselves; we are stewards and servants of the Lord, bought with a price.

> *"For ye are bought with a price: therefore glorify God in your body, and in your spirit, which are God's. Ye are bought with a price; be not ye the servants of men."*
> 1 Corinthians 6:20, 7:23

> *"Wherefore, my beloved, as ye have always obeyed, not as in my presence only, but now much more in my absence, work out your own salvation with fear and trembling. For it is God which worketh in you both to will and to do of his good pleasure."*
> Philippians 2:12-13

A steward, by definition, is dependent upon a continuous diet of spiritual food. For this reason, we as Christians congregate regularly to assure our spiritual growth and development. Failure to do so results in spiritual anemia. After enjoying a magnificent dinner, we do not conclude that because we are full, we do not need to eat again. The point is that a healthy diet lends itself to a healthy existence and a poor diet to ill health. As an essential part of the Church, we must seek the sincere milk[112] which comes through God's divine ministries at the hands of His anointed.[113] The Apostle Peter asserted that insufficient knowledge and understanding of God's word would contribute to the destruction of the unlearned.[114] This assertion demonstrates the magnitude of attending church with the distinct purpose of developing spiritual strength and potential.

---

111 Acts 20:28 Take heed therefore unto yourselves, and to all the flock, over the which the Holy Ghost hath made you overseers, to feed the Church of God, which he hath purchased with his own blood.
112 1 Peter 2:2 As newborn babes, desire the sincere milk of the word, that ye may grow thereby:
113 Hebrews 13:17 Obey them that have the rule over you, and submit yourselves: for they watch for your souls, as they that must give account, that they may do it with joy, and not with grief: for that is unprofitable for you.
114 2 Peter 3:16

Love, Obedience, and Works

Stewardship is about love. It is about willingly doing what is in your power to do. It is a product of one's conversion. Remember that conversion involves the surrender of man's will to God's and that it requires total commitment of the believer's personality, emotion and intellect. Our stewardship involves everything we do, and don't do and is thus the foundation of a believer's faithfulness to Christ. Being a servant of God is synonymous with being a giver. Take consolation in the fact that you cannot give materially until you have received, but we are all capable of showing love. This then is the importance of a professed stewardship. Paul wrote:

> *"For the love of Christ constraineth us; because we thus judge, that if one died for all, then were all dead: And that he died for all, that they which live should not henceforth live unto themselves, but unto him which died for them, and rose again."*
> 2 Corinthians 5:14-15

> *"But God be thanked, that ye were the servants of sin, but ye have obeyed from the heart that form of doctrine which was delivered you."*
> Romans 6:17

Our works begin with the word obedience. Being disobedient was the first sin committed by Adam and Eve. Our growth in this vital area of development begins when we become faithful to the various areas of service. The gospel is essential to the dynamics of salvation, instructions in righteousness, stewardship and the avoidance of many snares. Consider the following list of instructions taken directly from the bible. Use it as an aid to help you to reach your growth potential.

Become A Member of the Church	Acts 2:47
Attend Church As Regular As	Hebrews 10:25
Be Obedient as A Servant	Hebrews 13:17
Study God's Word	Jn 5:39, 2Tim 2:15 Acts 2:42
Become a Student of God's Word	Hebrews 5:12
Experience Personal Growth	I Co. 13:11

Be Strong	Rev. 2:10
Be Steadfast Unmovable	I Thes. 5:4-6 Eph. 3:1-7

Figure 3: Spiritual Growth

Taking the appropriate time to research and study these scriptures is a good start in demonstrating your obedience to the Bible's admonition to *"study and show thyself approved"*.[115] As you apply these scriptures, you will be converting your will to the will of the Lord as a good steward.

While our salvation is most assuredly permanent, we will still be judged by our "works", which is simply another term for stewardship. The only constructive work that we have is the work of the Lord. Such assurance can be seen in the request of the brothers James and John. They asked the Lord for seats of honor in His kingdom. Those disciples were unknowingly signing up for extreme suffering and persecution. The Lord did not deny their request. He told them of the prerequisite for that level. James was martyred (Acts 12:2). John was later exiled (Rev 1:9). From this we are informed of the consequences and rewards of stewardship. Like James and John, we are to be ready to accept the sword of death or the plow of long-suffering.

> ..."*can ye drink of the cup that I drink of? and be baptized with the baptism that I am baptized with?*"   Mark 10:38

> "*Know ye not, that to whom ye yield yourselves servants to obey, his servants ye are to whom ye obey; whether of sin unto death, or of obedience unto righteousness?*"   Romans 6:16

> "*Every man's work shall be made manifest: for the day shall declare it, because it shall be revealed by fire; and the fire shall try every man's work of what sort it is.*"   1 Corinthian. 3:13

The threefold purpose of the Church's ministry relates to leading, proclaiming, and caring. Pray over your usefulness and strive to exercise your gifts for the good of the church. There is surely a place for you. Will your works stand the test of fire, or will they go up in smoke-filled excuses, projections, and weak personal justifications?

---

115 2 Timothy 2:15

TITHING

The term "tithing" refers to the scriptural requirement of believers to surrender ten percent of all income to the mission of God. To tithe is to demonstrate one's faith, obedience, and acknowledgement of the fact that everything belongs to God and that all blessings come from Him. In the book of Malachi, the Lord accused His people of robbing Him. When they questioned how, He replied with "...*through tithes and offerings*".[116] Robbery is a violent crime. The definition of robbery is, "the act of unlawfully taking the property of another using violence or intimidation."[117] God's wrath was certainly apparent to His people. God said, *"Ye are cursed with a curse: for ye have robbed me, even this whole nation."*[118] As we shall see, God has required us to make this sacrifice that we might receive the greater blessing. What is the greater blessing? It is not stuff, things, or money. It is the power of faith working in the life of the believer.

A prevalent idea regarding the tithe is that we can forgo it altogether and instead, contribute our time to some noble cause. However, what makes the tithe unique is that it is a percentage of our resources and not our time.[119] This consideration logically raises the question, "Is the tithe a scriptural requirement from God?" This section will emphatically answer this question and discuss how pertinent it is to worship.

Although tithing is a material event, it has deep spiritual roots; meaning those who do it with the right heart condition, do it unconditionally because

---

116 Malachi 3:8 Will a man rob God? Yet ye have robbed me. But ye say, Wherein have we robbed thee? In tithes and offerings.
117 American Heritage Dictionary.
118 Malachi 3:9
119 Leviticus 27:30 And all the tithe of the land, whether of the seed of the land, or of the fruit of the tree, is the LORD'S: it is holy unto the LORD.

they wholeheartedly accredit God for everything they possess. Take for example, those who tithe obediently until their income increases significantly. With a larger income, they rationalize that it isn't necessary to pay such a large amount. Their conditional manner of obedience to the tithe demonstrates they were never true tithers. Large incomes tend to provoke a very human tendency to supplement our own worldly needs and desires with God's designated portion.[120] Since it is God who gives us all that we have, He is rightly grieved when we fail to acknowledge Him by giving back only a tenth of all that He has given to us.[121]

Long before ever becoming a codified law, the concept of the tithe was even evident in the Garden of Eden. Notice how God sealed the entrance to the *Tree of Life* after banishing Adam and Eve from the Garden. Compare it to the fact that He never blocked the entrance to the *Tree of the Knowledge of Good and Evil* while they resided within; surely He could have. But, had God not withheld something, then the couple wouldn't have had the opportunity to exercise a will, since nothing else was held back from them.

Abram, the father of faith, gave a tithe of all the spoils he gained when he came off victorious at the Battle of the Kings. His response to the victory was direct acknowledgement of the One who was truly responsible. Abram knew that God had given him the victory, and therefore he was willing to give only God the glory.[122]

> *And he blessed him, and said, Blessed be Abram of the most high God, possessor of heaven and earth: And blessed be the most high God, which hath delivered thine enemies into thy hand. And he gave him tithes of all.*   Genesis 14:19-20

Abram's grandson, Jacob, also made a vow which revealed his understanding of God's entitlement to the tithe. At Bethel, the House of God, Jacob met God and sanctified the place saying:

---

120 1 Timothy 6:10 For the love of money is the root of all evil: which while some coveted after, they have erred from the faith, and pierced themselves through with many sorrows.
121 Deuteronomy 8:18 But thou shalt remember the LORD thy God: for it is he that giveth thee power to get wealth, that he may establish his covenant which he sware unto thy fathers, as it is this day.
122 Genesis 14:22-23 And Abram said to the king of Sodom, I have lift up mine hand unto the LORD, the most high God, the possessor of heaven and earth, That I will not take from a thread even to a shoelatchet, and that I will not take any thing that is thine, lest thou shouldest say, I have made Abram rich:

> *If God will be with me, and will keep me in this way that I go, and will give me bread to eat, and raiment to put on, so that I come again to my father's house in peace; then shall the Lord be my God: And this stone, which I have set for a pillar, shall be God's house:* **and of all that thou shalt give me I will surely give the tenth unto thee.**
> Genesis 28:16-22

The Bible teaches that there are three things belonging solely to God. If God says "*it is Mine*"; the when, where, or why is irrelevant; "it" belongs to Him. How shrewd would it be to argue that God should not be given our first and our best? Have you ever thought about why Abel's offerings were pleasing to God while Cain's offerings were not? Cain gave to God, but he did not give his first. That response to God's requirement violated Cain's duty. The tithe is an intricate dedication that together with our willingness to put God first, constitutes acceptable devotion. The scripture below reveals these conditions to be equal in consideration to tithing.

Three things that belong solely to God:

1. *Only <u>the firstling</u> of the beasts, which should be the LORD'S firstling, no man shall sanctify it; whether it be ox, or sheep:* **it is the LORD'S.** ...
2. *<u>every devoted thing</u> is most holy unto the LORD.* ...
3. *<u>And all the tithe</u> of the land, whether of the seed of the land, or of the fruit of the tree, is the LORD'S: it is holy unto the LORD. And if a man will at all redeem ought of his tithes, he shall add thereto the fifth part thereof.* ...
Leviticus 27:26-34

Many presume that tithing is strictly an Old Testament Law. They are correct in that the tithe was in fact established in the Old Testament. Both Leviticus and Deuteronomy convey tithing as a legal requirement directly from Jehovah Himself. Did Christ abolish that law? Christ cautioned the Scribes and Pharisees because they were very particular about the tithe, yet careless with the weightier matters, such as, judgment, mercy, and faith.[123]

---

[123] *Matthew 23:23 Woe unto you, scribes and Pharisees, hypocrites! for ye pay tithe of mint and anise and cummin, and have omitted the weightier matters of the law, judgment, mercy, and faith:* **these ought ye to have done, and not to leave the other undone.**

The Lord concluded that they were correct in tithing, but incorrect in the administration of their caring ministry. Therefore we must conclude that regardless of which Testament; the tithe is His, and until He says that it is not, we are governed accordingly.

> *Thou shalt truly tithe all the increase of thy seed, that the field bringeth forth year by year.*   Deuteronomy 14:22

There are many instructions in the Old Testament that were meant specifically for the Jews; however the tithe is not one of them. The anointing of God resided with only select leaders during the era of the Old Testament. The general population responded to God with outward rituals and did so meticulously. How much more should we, being indwelled by the Holy Spirit, obediently acknowledge God with all our belongings?[124]

The personal acknowledgement that we are merely stewards over God's possessions is a serious matter. Adam was steward over the Garden; however he violated the instructions of the owner, God. This brought about the fall of man. On the other hand, Abraham was prepared to sacrifice his beloved and only son Isaac; recognizing that the boy was not necessarily *his* son, but God's.[125] Abraham's unwavering obedience and abundant blessings stand to remind us that we too, should be faithful stewards; always putting God's will first.[126]

As stewards, we are given the resources required to appropriately care for all that God has placed in our custody but we must be careful not to assume ownership of that which we do not own. For example, think of cashiers who daily manage money belonging to their employer. Each day the cash drawer is placed in their care, however there is never a question as to who truly owns and controls the money. The employee willingly complies with the reality that he or she has absolutely no authority over the money being collected. The owner, on the other hand, has no limitations to those resources. Remember, a steward is one who manages and cares for the affairs of another.

The tithe is an essential part of worship for another very important

---

124 Romans 8:9 But ye are not in the flesh, but in the Spirit, if so be that the Spirit of God dwell in you. Now if any man have not the Spirit of Christ, he is none of his.
125 Genesis 22:10 And Abraham stretched forth his hand, and took the knife to slay his son.
126 Romans 12:1 I beseech you therefore, brethren, by the mercies of God, that ye present your bodies a living sacrifice, holy, acceptable unto God, which is your reasonable service.

reason: it supports the Church; the visible representation of the invisible presence of our Lord. The Church's purpose is to declare the gospel to the entire world and to care for the poor and underprivileged. Her judgment shall encompass these responsibilities.

Our walk in Christ is truly a relationship. Each of us is responsible for the other. The tithe brings to fruition the phrase, *"Am I my brother's keeper?"* [127] One Hundred Thousand plus people are brought to Christ daily and are physically, mentally and spiritually enhanced by the ministries of churches all over the world. How are these churches financed? Through tithes and offerings. Love for God and for our neighbors is what compels true Christians to give freely, not grudgingly. They give because they recognize that God has given to them. They give proportionately because God taught them to do so through the Law. The Holy Ghost accelerates their desire to see men saved, and creates a spirit of willful giving to support the House of God.[128]

Some Christians refuse to give the tithe at their church because they disagree with how the funds will be used or perceive that their leaders already live too lavishly. Such ones should strongly consider joining another church so they can heed the biblical instruction to support the collective Church by giving God's things to God.[129] Jesus identified the apathy of His followers when He condemned them for neglecting His own needs. They were confused, reasoning that they had not seen Him in any of the predicaments that He referenced. They asked Him pointedly,

> *"...Lord, when saw we thee an hungred, or athirst, or a stranger, or naked, or sick, or in prison, and did not minister unto thee?"*

Jesus answered

> *"Verily I say unto you, Inasmuch as ye did it not to one of the least of these, ye did it not to me."*   Matthew 25:44, 45

---

[127] Genesis 4:9 And the LORD said unto Cain, Where is Abel thy brother? And he said, I know not: Am I my brother's keeper?
[128] Galatians 3:24-25 Wherefore the law was our schoolmaster to bring us unto Christ, that we might be justified by faith. But after that faith is come, we are no longer under a schoolmaster.
[129] Matthew 22:21 They say unto him, Caesar's. Then saith he unto them, Render therefore unto Caesar the things which are Caesar's; and unto God the things that are God's.

Many people believe that they are not financially able to tithe. They use the excuse that their bills already exceed their income so the tithe is not feasible for them. This is an unacceptable excuse for not tithing. In fact, not tithing may be directly responsible for many of the problems that negatively affect ones income and other issues in life.

After teaching a block of instruction in a New Members Class, I was confronted by a member who had serious apprehensions with the logic of tithing. The member wanted me to explain how God expected the tithe from a single parent with several children and an insufficient income. The member's countenance expressed great stress and concern. There was a side of me that could sympathize but sympathy was not what the situation called for. It was apparent that this person was being directed by the Spirit of the Lord to receive instructions on how to put God first and to receive His blessings. I attempted to resolve the matter by instructing them to be obedient with the little they did receive and to expect God to be faithful in a much larger way.[130]

The same day I had a scheduled meeting with the members of the Church's inner staff to discuss administrative responsibilities. With the particular member still on my mind, I asked the staff to consider allowing this person to reside, free of charge, in a very recent vacant dwelling owned by the church. The staff agreed to a one year minimum so that this member could gain control of their finances. Unfortunately, I never saw that member again. I can only imagine they left thinking that maybe the Church was only about taking, rather than giving to those truly in need. Because of the person's preoccupation with the concept of tithing, they missed out on a blessing that would have far exceeded the tenth being asked of them by God. If God needed help, He certainly would not look to us for it. Everything that God instructs us to do is for our benefit.

The Lord obviously does not need money. The fact is the money that we have is His. All of it! Without the Lord's giving, how could we have anything? It is unreasonable to think that Almighty God needs anything from us. God said:

---

[130] 2 Corinthians 9:7-8 Every man according as he purposeth in his heart, so let him give; not grudgingly, or of necessity: for God loveth a cheerful giver. And God is able to make all grace abound toward you; that ye, always having all sufficiency in all things, may abound to every good work:

"If I were hungry, I would not tell thee: for the world is mine, and the fullness thereof." (Psalm 50:12)

"The silver is mine, and the gold is mine, saith the Lord of hosts." (Haggai 2:8)

"For every beast of the forest is mine, and the cattle upon a thousand hills." (Psalm 50:10)

"And thou say in thine heart, My power and the might of mine hand hath gotten me this wealth. But thou shalt remember the Lord thy God: for it is he that giveth thee power to get wealth" (Deuteronomy 8:17-18)

The bible affirms the fact that a person's heart is represented by their treasure. Money supplies us with the resources that we need and desire. Why wouldn't God place Himself amidst our treasure?

"For where your treasure is, there will your heart be also." (Matthew 6:19-21).

No man can serve two masters: for either he will hate the one, and love the other; or else he will hold to the one, and despise the other. Ye cannot serve God and mammon.

Matthew 6:24

While tithing is a serious issue and a direct command from our Heavenly Father, it can neither afford nor cost a person's salvation. No, you won't be put out of the church or denied the gifts of ministry. Mishandling the tithe however, can impair our blessings on earth and reduce the abundance of our rewards in Heaven since being disobedient renders us subject to the curse of God.[131] Failing to tithe is equal to Adam and Eve eating from the forbidden tree. The fact that death accompanied their disobedience should not be seen as a penalty but a consequence for rejecting God's will.[132]

---

131 1 Timothy 6:10 For the love of money is the root of all evil: which while some coveted after, they have erred from the faith, and pierced themselves through with many sorrows.
132 Genesis 2:17 But of the tree of the knowledge of good and evil, thou shalt not eat of it: for in the day that thou eatest thereof thou shalt surely die.

Man has been given adequate knowledge and understanding to make good decisions in life. We have the freedom to do whatever we please, however we will surely give account for both our actions and inactions. Abram, Isaac and Jacob all acknowledged God by attributing all their wealth to Him. How do you acknowledge Him? Some of us would like to think that we can acknowledge God anyway we see fit. Imagine trying to depart from a barbershop or salon with that same mindset; that you can pay the barber or stylist whatever you decide the service is worth. On the contrary, most of us not only pay the posted price, but we also give a tip. This "tip" would be synonymous with the offering which we will discuss next.

OFFERINGS

It has been said that God does not develop gifts, but that He develops givers instead. God created everything that we call blessings before He created us. The offering is a monetary gift from the believer to the Church that comes from the ninety percent remaining of a person's income after having given the tithe. The ability to give offerings reveals even more clearly the blessings that God bestows. Think about it, in order for us to be givers we must have already been blessed with gifts. Who gets the credit for those conditions; you or God? Your answer is in your giving. Whenever we give in accordance to God's directions, we in effect, give Him the credit. When we don't give accordingly; we take the credit for ourselves.

Christians often confuse their desire to assist the homeless or to support their favorite charity with tithing. It is not from the tithe, but the offering that we provide for these extended ministries. With the offering, you have the discretion to determine who receives it and for what purpose it will be used.

The house of the Lord is the place designated by God to represent the presence of His Spirit. In the Old Testament, it was the Temple. The New Testament House of God is the Church. Each represents the presence of God, the symbol of redemption, and the place of worship. Therefore, God still maintains a visible house among men, and men are instructed to maintain support of that house. When the Church closes her doors, the hungry perish; the naked are abused; and the jailed are comfortless. When you elect not to give, then you cast your vote to close the doors of the Church.

Sins of every category have been forgiven of God. Yet, the New Testament records that the Holy Ghost attributes monetary sins, as in the case of Judas Iscariot and Ananias and Sapphira, worthy of instant death. Judas is called a devil because he threw his lot in with Satan to gain silver. Ananias was asked of Peter, "why hath Satan filled thine heart to lie to the Holy Ghost?"[133] Notice that unwillingness to forego monetary gain for the sake of the Kingdom is closely associated with Satan.

Tithes and offerings are the visible means of support for the Church and ministries; not dues, chicken dinners, special programs, or sponsors. God's plan works! God Himself said,

> *"prove me, (try me) . . . if I will not open you the windows of heaven, and pour you out a blessing, that there shall not be room enough to receive it."*   Malachi 3:10

The Lord promises to take care of His people. Jesus told us to take no thought for what we shall eat, drink, or be clothed with. He knows that we need these things, and assures us that seeking first the Kingdom of God and His righteousness ensures that all of our needs will be provided for.[134] Those who are faithful in giving are personally aware of the abundance of the blessings that they receive from God. These blessings do not always appear in monetary form. Our health, employment and the welfare of our love ones rate high on the scale of peace, and fulfillment.

> *"And all nations shall call you blessed: for ye shall be a delightsome land . . .*   (Malachi 3:12)."

Most parents are very concerned about the amount of resources they will leave to their children when they depart this earth. After all, they inherited our looks, habits, and often even our attitude. Those who do not honor God with their abundance have left to their progenitors a contaminated resource that will never be the blessing that it could have otherwise been. You and I were born sinners because of the disobedience of Adam and Eve. We cannot prevent the same for our children but we can minimize their plight by leading them by example. Since God's kingdom will outlast any resources you may accumulate in this life, make sure that God's will is the most important aspect of your estate.

---

133 John 6:70; Luke 22:3; Acts 5:3
134 Matthew 6:31-34

THE CHURCH

As we conclude our orientation to this new relationship and fellowship with Christ, we must examine the organism in which these truths are kept.

The Church is the manifestation of God's redemptive power. The bible gives us a bird's eye view of the inaugural birth of the Church during Pentecost; the Church was born in the Upper Room.[135] Before the baptism in the Holy Ghost, the disciples were scattered. After having received the Holy Ghost, they became one. By the Power of God, the Holy Ghost, they were indwelled and regenerated. One hundred and twenty others were on hand with the Apostles to experience this miraculous occurrence. Peter preached the first sermon and 3,000 souls were added.[136] This marked the infancy of the personification of the Lord's body and bride. She spoke in the languages of all nations and the message was the same; "Jesus is Lord."

These facts illustrate to us that the Church is not a building or an organization. She is not something that man can alter. Most often, when we refer to our local church we speak of "joining" the church's membership. In the greater sense of acknowledgment, we do not join God's Church, we are born into it. It is for this reason that every conscientious congregation will examine prospective members to assure that they are saved prior to granting membership. Because the Church is an organism, not an institution, people cannot join her, leave her, only to rejoin her again.

The bible frequently references the Church as the body of the Lord. This metaphor allows us to easily imagine the many different, but essential parts that the body has; the eye, the ear, the mouth etc. Which of these parts can be joined to the body individually? The body is intact at birth. As the body

---

135 Acts 2:1-13
136 Acts 2:41

of Christ, we can no more "join" the Church than we can join an arm to our body. The Church consists of live, warm bodies that are empowered by the Holy Spirit to make up the only true body of the Lord. For this to occur, we must all be born again.

The scriptures also confirm that the Church is not the result of haphazard circumstances. She cannot be attributed to evolution or some unknown form of mutation, but the plan of God from the very beginning. When Jesus said, "*Upon this rock I will build my Church,*" He was giving His disciples a lesson on the destiny of His presence on earth.[137] The Church is the embodiment of Jesus empowered by the Holy Spirit. Although she was revealed after Israel, the Church *preceded* Israel according to the scripture. Both Israel and the nations (from whom came the Church) originated with the foundation of the world, while the Church existed before the world began. In order to comprehend this, one simply needs to recognize that the bible categorizes people into three groups. They are the Jews, the Gentiles, and the Church.[138] The last of the three groups to be revealed was actually the first to be founded.

The following scriptures reveal the Church in light of eternity, prior to her presence on earth:

1. "*According as he hath chosen us in him before the foundation of the world, that we should be holy and without blame before him in love… Having predestined us unto the adoption of children by Jesus Christ to himself, according to the good pleasure of his will.*"
   Ephesians 1:4-5.

2. "*But we speak the wisdom of God in a mystery, even the hidden wisdom, which God ordained before the world unto our glory.*"
   1 Corinthians 2:7.

3. "*Who hath saved us, and called us with a holy calling, not according to our works, but according to his own purpose and grace, which was given us in Christ Jesus before the world began.*"
   2 Timothy 1:9…

---

137 Matthew 16:18 And I say also unto thee, That thou art Peter, and upon this rock I will build my Church; and the gates of hell shall not prevail against it.
138 1 Corinthian 10:32

4. *"Elect according to the <u>foreknowledge of</u> obedience and sprinkling of the blood of Jesus Christ"*   1 Peter 1: 2,

Before the coming of Christ, the true notion of "Church" was inconceivable until Jesus Himself spoke it into existence, thereby empowering it. To understand the Church requires one to understand the essence of being born again which was impossible prior to Jesus' presence on earth.[139] Since Christ is the literal head of the Church, prior to His birth, death, and resurrection, any mention of the Church would have revealed a headless body.

Jesus facilitated our ability to become a Church by paying the ransom price.

"Joining" the largest, most popular Church in town assures you of nothing. Being born again secures your position within the Church of Jesus Christ. This Church is the spiritual body of the Lord; His bride who awaits His return.[140] Jesus loves you so much that He died for you.[141] You must accept that God raised Him from the dead for you.[142] You can receive Him into your heart by sincerely asking:[143]

"Jesus I am a sinner and I submit to you.[144] Take me as I am, and make me that which you desire me to be.[145] I love you, Lord,[146] and I receive you now by faith.[147] I believe

---

139 Ephesians 5:23: For the husband is the head of the wife, even as Christ is the head of the Church: and he is the saviour of the body.(See also 1 Corinthians 12:27)
140 Ephesians 5:27 That he might present it to himself a glorious church, not having spot, or wrinkle, or any such thing; but that it should be holy and without blemish.
141 Romans 5:8 But God commendeth his love toward us, in that, while we were yet sinners, Christ died for us.
142 Romans 10:9 That if thou shalt confess with thy mouth the Lord Jesus, and shalt believe in thine heart that God hath raised him from the dead, thou shalt be saved.
143 Matthew 7:7 Ask, and it shall be given you; seek, and ye shall find; knock, and it shall be opened unto you:
144 Luke 18:17 Verily I say unto you, Whosoever shall not receive the kingdom of God as a little child shall in no wise enter therein.
145 1 Timothy 1:15 This is a faithful saying, and worthy of all acceptation, that Christ Jesus came into the world to save sinners; of whom I am chief.
146 Mark 12:30 And thou shalt love the Lord thy God with all thy heart, and with all thy soul, and with all thy mind, and with all thy strength: this is the first commandment.
147 Revelation 3:20 Behold, I stand at the door, and knock: if any man hear my voice, and open the door, I will come in to him, and will sup with him, and he with me.

that you died to pay for my sins and that you rose to give me everlasting life.[148] **You are my Lord and my God."**[149]

Words such as these spoken from a sincere heart are the only way to become a member of *the Church*.[150]

---

148 1 Corinthians 15:3 For I delivered unto you first of all that which I also received, how that Christ died for our sins according to the scriptures;
149 John 20:28 And Thomas answered and said unto him, My Lord and my God.
150 Romans 10:13 For whosoever shall call upon the name of the Lord shall be saved.

CHURCH ADMINISTRATION

Government, by divine authority, is the responsibility to care for God's creation.[151] There are several different types of government. Although the word government is often associated with politics, we will now discuss examples of government in terms of the Church. The three examples we will consider are the Episcopal (monocratic-autocracy), the Presbyterian (aristocratic-oligarchy), and the Congregational (democratic) forms of government. It is not uncommon to find small traces of one particular style intertwined with another category, however a church will normally represent its central belief system through its organizational structure. For this reason, we will consider each class based on its dominant attributes.

AUTOCRACY

An autocracy is a system of government in which supreme political power to direct all the activities of the state is concentrated in the hands of one person, whose decisions are subject to neither external legal restraints nor regularized mechanisms of popular control (except perhaps for the implicit threat of coup d'état or mass insurrection).[152] The Catholic Church is the best example of religious autocracy because its members have assigned the Pope supreme control of all the organization's religious considerations.

---

151 Romans 13:1-2 Let every soul be subject unto the higher powers. For there is no power but of God: the powers that be are ordained of God. Whosoever therefore resisteth the power, resisteth the ordinance of God: and they that resist shall receive to themselves damnation.
152 From Wikipedia, the free encyclopedia

CATHOLIC

The title "Pope" stems from the Greek word *papas*, which simply means "father." Early in Christian history it was used as a formal title expressing affectionate respect for any bishop and sometimes even priests. Today it continues to be used in Eastern Orthodox Churches for the patriarch of Alexandria.

In the West, however, it has been used exclusively as a technical title for the bishop of Rome and head of the Roman Catholic Church since about the ninth century — but not for solemn occasions. Technically, the person holding the office of the bishop of Rome and Pope also has the titles:

Holy Father
His Holiness
Bishop of Rome
Vicar of Jesus Christ
Successor of St. Peter
Prince of the Apostles
Supreme Pontiff of the Universal Church
Primate of Italy
Patriarch of the West
Servant of the Servants of God
Archbishop and Metropolitan of the Province of Rome
Sovereign of the State of Vatican City

A pope is, in essence, the supreme legislative, executive, and judicial authority in the Roman Catholic Church — there are no "checks and balances" like one may be accustomed to finding in secular governments. Canon 331 describes the office of pope thus:

The office uniquely committed by the Lord to Peter, the first of the Apostles, and to be transmitted to his successors, abides in the Bishop of the Church of Rome. He is head of the College of Bishops, the Vicar of Christ, and the Pastor of the universal Church here on earth. Consequently, by virtue of his office, he has supreme, full, immediate, and universal ordinary power in the Church, and he can always freely exercise this power.

A pope (abbreviated PP.) is chosen by majority vote in the College of Cardinals, the member of which were themselves appointed by the previous pope(s). To win election, a person must get at least two-thirds of the votes cast. Cardinals stand just below the pope in terms of power and authority in the Church hierarchy.

Candidates do not have to be from the College of Cardinals or even a Catholic — technically, anyone at all can be chosen. However, candidates have almost always been a cardinal or bishop, especially in modern history.

Doctrinally, the pope is regarded as the successor of St. Peter, leader of the apostles after the death and resurrection of Jesus Christ. This is an important factor in the tradition that the pope is believed to have jurisdiction over the entire Christian Church in matters of faith, morals and Church government. This doctrine is known as *papal primacy*.

Although papal primacy is based partially on the role of Peter in the New Testament, this theological factor is not the only relevant issue. Another, equally important, factor is the historical role of both the Roman Church in religious matters and the city of Rome in temporal matters. Thus, the notion of papal primacy has not been one which existed for the earliest Christian communities; rather, it developed as the Christian Church itself developed. Catholic Church doctrine has always been based partly upon scripture and partly upon evolving Church traditions, and this is simply another example of that fact.

Papal primacy has long been a significant obstacle to ecumenical efforts among the various Christian Churches. Most Eastern Orthodox Christians, for example, would be quite willing to accord the Roman bishop the same respect, deference and authority as is accorded to any Eastern Orthodox patriarch — but that is not the same as granting the Roman pope special authority over **all** Christians. A great many Protestants are quite willing to grant the pope a position of special moral leadership, however any more formal authority than that would conflict with the Protestant ideal that there can be no intermediaries between a Christian and God.[153]

OLOGARCHY

Oligarchy (from Greek ὀλιγαρχία, oligarkhía) is a form of power structure in which power effectively rests with an elite class distinguished by royalty, wealth, family ties, commercial, and/or military legitimacy. The word oligarchy is derived from the Greek words "ὀλίγος" (olígos), "a few" and the verb "ἄρχω" (archo), "to rule, to govern, to command".[154]

---

153 ©2012 About.com. All rights reserved
154 From Wikipedia, the free encyclopedia

PRESBYTERIAN

The name "Presbyterian" comes from the word "presbyter" meaning "elder." Presbyterian Churches have a representational form of Church government, in which authority is given to elected lay leaders (elders). These lay elders work together with the Church's ordained minister. The governing body of an individual Presbyterian congregation is called a session. Several sessions constitute a presbytery, several presbyteries make up a synod, and the General Assembly oversees the entire denomination.[155]

CONGREGATIONAL

Congregational Churches are Protestant Christian Churches practicing Congregationalist Church governance, in which each congregation independently and autonomously runs its own affairs. Many Congregational Churches claim their descent from a family of Protestant denominations formed on a theory of union published by the theologian Robert Browne in 1592. These arose from the Nonconformist religious movement during the Puritan reformation of the Church of England. In Great Britain, the early Congregationalists were called separatists or independents to distinguish them from the similarly Calvinistic Presbyterians. Some Congregationalists in Britain still call themselves Independent. Congregational Churches were widely established in the Massachusetts Bay Colony, later New England.[156]

BAPTICOSTALS (BAPTIST-PENTECOSTALS AND OTHERS)

Baptists are Christians who comprise a group of denominations and Churches that subscribe to a doctrine that baptism should be performed only for professing believers (believer's baptism, as opposed to infant baptism), and that it must be done by immersion (as opposed to affusion or sprinkling). Other tenets of Baptist Churches include soul competency (liberty), salvation through faith alone, scripture alone as the rule of faith and practice, and the autonomy of the local congregation. Baptists recognize two ministerial offices, pastors and deacons. Baptist Churches

---

155 ©2012 About.com. All rights reserved
156 From Wikipedia, the free encyclopedia

are widely considered to be Protestant Churches, though some Baptists disavow this identity.

Diverse from their beginning, those identifying as Baptists today differ widely from one another in what they believe, how they worship, their attitudes toward other Christians, and their understanding of what is important in Christian discipleship.

Historians trace the earliest Baptist Church back to 1609 in Amsterdam, with English Separatist John Smyth as its pastor. In accordance with his reading of the New Testament, he rejected baptism of infants and instituted baptism only of believing adults. Baptist practice spread to England, where the General Baptists considered Christ's atonement to extend to all people, while the Particular Baptists believed that it extended only to the elect. In 1638, Roger Williams established the first Baptist congregation in the North American colonies. In the mid-18th century, the First Great Awakening increased Baptist growth in both New England and the South. The Second Great Awakening in the South in the early 19th century increased Church membership, as did the preachers' lessening of support for abolition and manumission of slavery, which had been part of the 18th-century teachings. Baptist missionaries have spread their Church to every continent.

The Baptist World Alliance reports more than 41 million members in more than 150,000 congregations. In 2002, there were over 100 million Baptists and Baptistic group members worldwide and over 33 million in North America. The largest Baptist association is the Southern Baptist Convention, with over 16 million members.[157]

Before becoming a part of a particular congregation we should assure ourselves as much as possible that we are in total agreement with its doctrines. The bible teaches that two cannot walk together except they agree.[158]

---

157 From Wikipedia, the free encyclopedia
158 Amos 3:3 Can two walk together, except they be agreed?

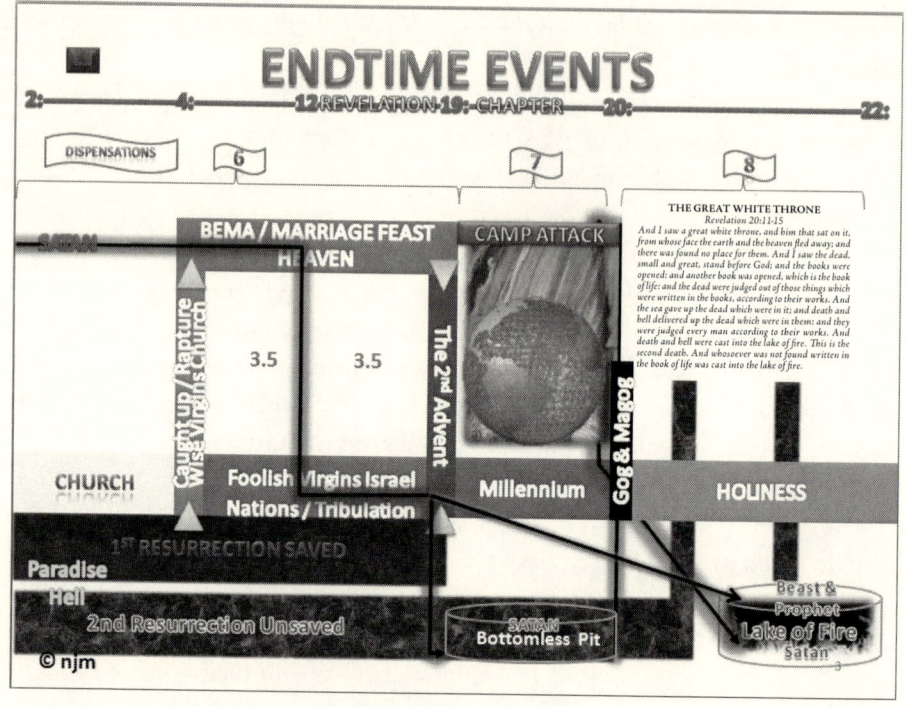

Figure 4 End Time Events

1. THE CHURCH AND COMPETING RELIGIONS
2. THE RAPTURE LEADING TO THE BEMA & MARRIAGE FEAST
3. THE TRIBULATION & THE EVANGELIZATION OF THE NATIONS
4. SECOND ADVENT, ARMAGEDDON, JUDGMENT OF THE NATIONS
5. ANTICHRIST & FALSE PROPHET LAKE OF FIRE, SATAN/PIT
6. THE MILLENNIUM KINGDOM
7. SATAN RELEASED FROM THE PIT, GOG & MAGOG
8. THE ATTACK OF THE CAMP OF GOD
9. THE CLEANSING OF THE WORLD AND ANNIHILATION OF EVIL
10. THE WHITE THRONE JUDGMENT
11. DEATH, HELL, AND THE HOST OF EVIL INTO THE LAKE OF FIRE
12. THE PERFECT KINGDOM

ESCHATOLOGY

Eschatology is the study of the final events that will take place as the world winds down to a close. The chart on the previous page will help you to follow the bible's prophesy of the events that shall come.

Notice the row of flags on the chart beginning with the number six and ending with the number eight. The brackets below these flags mark the associated dispensation. A dispensation can be described as an economy; it is defined as a time period or situation where God dealt with people based on His requirements which varied from one time period to the next. For example, during the dispensation of law, the Lord required continual sacrifices however, in the dispensation of grace, only one sacrifice was required. There are eight dispensations in all. Up to this point we have only discussed events relative to the sixth dispensation-the Dispensation of Grace, in which we currently live. This dispensation began with the resurrection of our Lord Jesus.

The sixth dispensation is sometimes called the ecumenical dispensation referring to the conglomerate society of the world's religions. Although there are at least seven major religions competing for acceptance, there can be only one that is true. The true religion is Christianity; the acknowledgment of Jesus as Christ, the Son of the Living God; God in the Flesh. The greatest contender of this fact is the Jewish Nation.[159] The Jews are destined to come to this glorious truth during the end of this dispensation, in the period known as Tribulation. It should also be noted that all the nations will, during the same event, Tribulation, come to know Jesus as God. The true battle has

---

159 John 10:33 The Jews answered him, saying, For a good work we stone thee not; but for blasphemy; and because that thou, being a man, makest thyself God.

never been between God and man; it is between God and Satan and all those who choose to follow him.[160]

The bible maps the events that will lead up to the destruction of Satan and his intentions. These confirmations should reassure us in our everyday challenges that the battle is already won. There are no acceptable excuses for spiritual ignorance.[161]

The Rapture and the Left Behind

The bible repeatedly heralds of an impending "rapture" for which we should always be on the watch. We are explicitly warned that some will be caught up while others will be left behind.[162] The Rapture is a future event where the Church will be caught up to meet the Lord in the sky.[163] It will encapsulate not only the Church, but also all of the world's children who have not yet reached the age of accountability. Imagine the power of the message associated with this sudden disappearance. Their absence will confirm the Lord's Word. It will be the burning desire to understand this phenomenon that will lead many of the lost ones who never had the opportunity before, to come to the knowledge of the saving grace of Jesus.[164]

The Church and Israel

The book of Matthew chapter 25 gives a parable of ten virgins awaiting a bridegroom; five of them are wise, and five are foolish. The distinction between the wise and foolish virgins is the oil that provided the fuel for the light of their lamps. The oil symbolizes the Holy Ghost, which reveals the

---

160 Matthew 25:41 Then shall he say also unto them on the left hand, Depart from me, ye cursed, into everlasting fire, prepared for the devil and his angels:
161 Romans 1:20 For the invisible things of him from the creation of the world are clearly seen, being understood by the things that are made, even his eternal power and Godhead; so that they are without excuse:
162 Matthew 24:40,41: Then shall two be in the field; the one shall be taken, and the other left. Two women shall be grinding at the mill; the one shall be taken, and the other left.
163 1 Thessalonians 4:16-17 For the Lord himself shall descend from heaven with a shout, with the voice of the archangel, and with the trump of God: and the dead in Christ shall rise first: Then we which are alive and remain shall be caught up together with them in the clouds, to meet the Lord in the air: and so shall we ever be with the Lord.
164 Matthew 18:3 And said, Verily I say unto you, Except ye be converted, and become as little children, ye shall not enter into the kingdom of heaven.

truth of Jesus as God. The five wise virgins represent the Church. Orthodox Jews are the foolish virgins who continue to deny the deity of Christ. Their denial is divine since the bible teaches that their ignorance is for the blessing of the Gentiles.[165] Just as the bridegroom arrives while the foolish virgins are out shopping for oil, Israel will still be out looking for God when He returns and closes the door. *"Except a man be born again, he cannot see the Kingdom of God"* are the words of Jesus Himself.[166] Jesus also said that "He came unto His own and that His own received Him not". Their rejection of Him certainly branded them as "foolish". For this reason, the foolish virgins (Jews) will enter into tribulation. It will be during the tribulation that they will finally accept Jesus as their Lord.[167]

> *He came unto his own, and his own received him not. But as many as received him, to them gave he power to become the sons of God, even to them that believe on his name: Which were born, not of blood, nor of the will of the flesh, nor of the will of man, but of God.*   John 1:11-13

The Bema and Tribulation

The Bema Judgment is the judgment of the Church; this is where the saints will receive their rewards.[168] This judgment is the judgment of works which the Church is subject to in heaven.[169] The tribulation will simultaneously be taking place on earth. Three and a half years into the tribulation, Satan

---

165 Romans 11:11, 25:I say then, Have they stumbled that they should fall? God forbid: but [rather] through their fall salvation [is come] unto the Gentiles, for to provoke them to jealousy. (25) For I would not, brethren, that ye should be ignorant of this mystery, lest ye should be wise in your own conceits; that blindness in part is happened to Israel, until the fulness of the Gentiles be come in.
166 John 3:3
167 Revelations 14:4: These are they which were not defiled with women; for they are virgins. These are they which follow the Lamb whithersoever he goeth. These were redeemed from among men, being the firstfruits unto God and to the Lamb.
168 2 Corinthians 5:10: For we must all appear before the judgment seat of Christ; that every one may receive the things done in his body, according to that he hath done, whether it be good or bad.
169 1 Corinthians 3:13 Every man's work shall be made manifest: for the day shall declare it, because it shall be revealed by fire; and the fire shall try every man's work of what sort it is.

will be permanently cast out of heaven down to the earth.[170] He will join his unholy comrades, the Antichrist and the False prophet. The final three and a half years will be so horrific it is called, "The Great Tribulation".[171] As pain and suffering increase on earth, the Church will be advancing towards the marriage feast in heaven.[172] The marriage feast is the consummation of the Bride of Christ, His body.[173]

The First Resurrection and the Judgment of the Nations Armageddon

At the end of the seven years of tribulation, Jesus will return to earth. When He returns, His Church and the souls of the martyrs (those killed after having accepted Jesus during tribulation) will accompany Him.[174] The catastrophic events to follow His return are often referred to as Armageddon. First, the Antichrist and the False prophet will be cast into the Lake of Fire.[175] Satan will then be locked into the bottomless pit and there will be massive destruction of those who joined the assault on God and or His people.[176]

The souls of the martyrs who accompany the Lord will receive their resurrected bodies at this time. The Lord will judge all living beings upon His return, separating them as sheep and goats. The sheep are the people He will lead into the Millennium Kingdom (Dispensation 7).The goats are the people who are condemned to death and are awaiting the second resurrection (Matt 25:34, 41). The bible references several different resurrection events yet only names two categorically; the first and the second resurrections. There is much confusion surrounding this discussion because there are several separate

---

[170] Revelation 12:9 And the great dragon was cast out, that old serpent, called the Devil, and Satan, which deceiveth the whole world: he was cast out into the earth, and his angels were cast out with him.

[171] Matthew 24:21 For then shall be great tribulation, such as was not since the beginning of the world to this time, no, nor ever shall be.

[172] Revelation 19:7-8 Let us be glad and rejoice, and give honour to him: for the marriage of the Lamb is come, and his wife hath made herself ready. And to her was granted that she should be arrayed in fine linen, clean and white: for the fine linen is the righteousness of saints.

[173] Ephesians 5:23 For the husband is the head of the wife, even as Christ is the head of the church: and he is the saviour of the body.

[174] Revelation 19:11

[175] Revelation 19:20

[176] Revelation 20:3; Revelation 19:15

events which collectively constitute the first resurrection. Jesus' resurrection, the resurrection of the Old Testament saints, and the future resurrection of both the Church and of the martyrs, are all a part of the first resurrection. Each resurrection prior to the millennium is a part of the first resurrection (Rev 20:6).

The Millennium
The Righteous Dispensation

All of the covenants that God made with Israel during their earthly pilgrimage will be fulfilled during the Millennium. Finally, the House of Israel will acknowledge that their King has always been King Jesus; the only one worthy to sit on the throne of His people (1Cor 10:2-5).

The eleventh chapter of Isaiah describes the level of peace that will be experienced throughout the Millennium Reign. Satan will be imprisoned and the antichrist and false prophet will already be in the Lake of Fire during this euphoric period. (Rev. 20:2, 19:20). In the absence of the unholy trio, the power of sin (death) will be suspended.

Gog and Magog

At the end of the millennium, Satan will be loosed from his prison. He will then commence to gathering a large army from the masses of people born during the thousand years.[177] On your chart this is depicted as Gog and Magog. It should also be noted that anyone born during the Millennium who accepts Jesus as their Lord, will be translated immediately following that event. Translation is the phenomenon whereby a person goes from life in the flesh directly to life in the spirit, without ever experiencing death.

Resurrection and Translation

Clues to the mystery of God's plan for the saved were woven into the scriptures' account of the first two natural deaths. However, the mystery could not be unraveled for eons.

From the events of Eden, death became the enemy of all men.[178] Before

---

177 Revelation 20:7-10
178 1 Corinthians 15:26 The last enemy that shall be destroyed is death.

Jesus, Paradise was the holding place of the souls that departed from the earth.[179] Paradise remained in the heart of the earth until after Jesus' resurrection.[180] At which time He took Paradise to its rightful home in heaven.[181] Immediately following this historic event, Jesus returned to the earth and was seen on several occasions by His disciples.[182] His final ascension to heaven was by means of translation.[183] Jesus' personal resurrection and translation ensures saints of our ability, through the Holy Ghost, to be with the Lord when we depart from this earth.[184]

For the saints of God, translation is the only other means of departing the earth. Translation was first recorded relative to Enoch's departure.[185] Enoch was the seventh generation of those who called on the name of the Lord. The number seven in this case is synonymous with Sabbath, a period of rest. This period is today referred to as the Millennium. Just as Enoch, the seventh generation, was translated so will all the saints who will be born during the Millennium, the seventh dispensation. The translation was also witnessed in the departure of Elijah. He was chosen by God to complement Moses in the witnessing of God's power. Moses is the assurance of the resurrection while Elijah is the assurance of the translation. Jesus told His disciples that He is the resurrection and the life.[186] As the resurrection, Jesus is the way for all who taste death. As the life, He is the way for all those who are translated. In either case, the saints are given the assurance that nothing will separate us from being at home with the Lord.

---

179 Luke 23:43 And Jesus said unto him, Verily I say unto thee, To day shalt thou be with me in paradise.
180 Matthew 27:52-53 And the graves were opened; and many bodies of the saints which slept arose, And came out of the graves after his resurrection, and went into the holy city, and appeared unto many.
181 2 Corinthians 12:4 How that he was caught up into paradise, and heard unspeakable words, which it is not lawful for a man to utter.
182 John 20:26 And after eight days again his disciples were within, and Thomas with them: then came Jesus, the doors being shut, and stood in the midst, and said, Peace be unto you.
183 Acts 1:9 And when he had spoken these things, while they beheld, he was taken up; and a cloud received him out of their sight.
184 2 Corinthians 5:8 We are confident, I say, and willing rather to be absent from the body, and to be present with the Lord.
185 Genesis 5:24; Hebrews 11:5; Jude 1:14
186 John 11:25, 26

The White Throne Judgment of The Unsaved

Satan's release from the bottomless abyss will mark the end of the Millennium. Upon his release, those who join Satan in the attack of God's camp will be killed by fire from heaven and immediately brought before the White Throne Judgment.[187] The graves of the dead will be opened and the unsaved will resurrect into bodies of flesh.[188] They will be judged from the very book (the bible) that introduced them to Jesus and His love. When Jesus came to save them they refused Him, but when He comes to judge them they will not have the option to deny Him again. They will individually be sentenced to their destination in the lake of fire. This damnation is called the second death since they will be killed again in the flesh.[189] If I may add, the only consolation for those who will spend eternity in damnation is this: during their lives, most were never high enough to personally meet Satan and during their torment, they will never be low enough. Satan will probably be surrounded by angels who will fault him for all eternity.[190]

New Jerusalem
The Holy Dispensation

Finally, the Lord will cleanse the earth by fire and remove heaven from its foundation.[191] This will mark the beginning of the final dispensation; the dispensation of Holiness. The eighth dispensation is to dispensations, what the eighth day is to believers. Jesus' resurrection occurred on the eighth day (the first day after the seventh day). On the eighth day, Jesus delivered the deadly blow to death and solidified everlasting life. The eighth dispensation will not be encumbered with sin's presence, power, or penalty. It is the dispensation of eternal life for all who shall enter therein. New Jerusalem will visibly descend as a bride adorned for her husband.[192] The new city of God's people is described as having twelve gates of pearls named after the twelve tribes of Israel and twelve foundations each bearing the name of one of the twelve apostles of Christ, representing the final consummation of all

---

187 Revelation 20:9
188 Revelation 20:13
189 Revelaion 2:11, 20:6,14, 21:8
190 Isaiah 14:19,20
191 2 Peter 3:10
192 Revelation 21:2

God's people.[193] God and His people will be eternally undisturbed by any force.

The Abdication of the Earthly Throne

It is during this time that Jesus abdicates the throne of "The God Man", and brings to fruition the very presence of Almighty God. [194] This is the teaching that discloses the reality that there is but one God albeit we have by necessity come to know Him through a triune presence. In the war of time, God manifested Himself in flesh and in Spirit. In flesh, He conquered the enemy of death, and in the Spirit He empowered everlasting life. While accomplishing both of these requirements He continued to reign in heaven and to direct the course of all existence. Such a mighty feat has caused many to deny His presence in these different capacities at the same time. Such is the consideration of those who attempt to attribute human limitations to Almighty God.[195]

Yes, there is a future period when God will encompass His fullness,[196] and therefore no distinction of personality or manifestation. This is the period that Paul was referencing when he said

"For now we see through a glass, darkly; but then face to face: now I know in part; but then shall I know even as also I am known."
1 Corinthians 13:12

Heaven Is the Destination for God's People
Jesus Is the Way

---

193 Revelation 21:12,14
194 1 Corinthians 15:28; 1 Timothy 6:15,16
195 Isaiah 55:8-9 For my thoughts are not your thoughts, neither are your ways my ways, saith the LORD. For as the heavens are higher than the earth, so are my ways higher than your ways, and my thoughts than your thoughts.
196 Romans 1:20 For the invisible things of him from the creation of the world are clearly seen, being understood by the things that are made, even his eternal power and Godhead; so that they are without excuse:

DISPENSATIONS 6-8

(Economies)

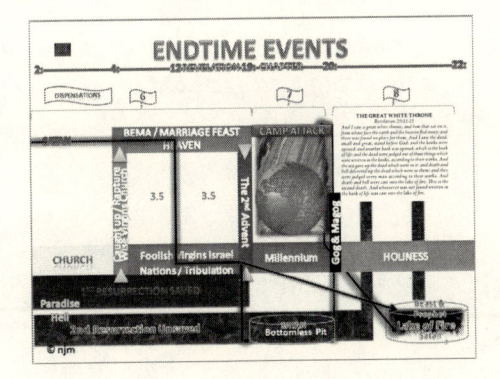

The Church

Jesus answered, Verily, verily, I say unto thee, Except a man be born of water and of the Spirit, he cannot enter into the kingdom of God. **John 3:5**

And I say also unto thee, That thou art Peter, and upon this rock I will build my church; and the gates of hell shall not prevail against it. **Matthew 16:18**

Take heed therefore unto yourselves, and to all the flock, over the which the Holy Ghost hath made you overseers, to feed the church of God, which he hath purchased with his own blood. **Acts 20:28**

And he is the head of the body, the church: who is the beginning, the firstborn from the dead; that in all things he might have the preeminence. **Colossians 1:18**

For the husband is the head of the wife, even as Christ is the head of the church: and he is the saviour of the body. Therefore as the church is subject unto Christ, so let the wives be to their own husbands in every thing. **Ephesians 5:23-24**

That he might present it to himself a glorious church, not having spot, or wrinkle, or any such thing; but that it should be holy and without blemish. **Ephesians 5:27**

Then we which are alive and remain shall be caught up together with them in the clouds, to meet the Lord in the air: and so shall we ever be with the Lord. **1 Thessalonians 4:17**

QUESTIONS AND ANSWERS
The Church

1. **Q.** Is the word "church" the place that many Christians go to worship?
   A. The word "church" comes from the Greek word ekklesia which is defined as "an assembly" or "called-out ones." The root meaning of "church" is not that of a building, but of people. (Matt 18:20)

2. **Q.** Some believe that Peter's response to the Lord's question "... *Whom do men say that I the Son of man am? (Matthew 16:13)* became the foundation of the church. His response was *"Thou art the Christ, the Son of the living God". (Matthew 16:18)* Jesus stated... *"And I say also unto thee, That thou art Peter, and upon this rock I will build my church; and the gates of hell shall not prevail against it." (Matthew 16:16)* Did the Lord imply that the church was to be built on the Apostle Peter?
   A. No, Peter's response was the personal acknowledgment of Jesus being the Christ, the Son (manifestation, 1 Tim. 3:16) of God, that's the foundation for all believers. (Matt 16:16)

3. **Q.** Why wasn't the church mentioned by name in the Old Testament since it is the heart of the New Testament?
   A. The church is the body of the Lord and without the Lord it would have appeared headless. Jesus had to appear first and then the body. The Old Testament is about the Saviour and not the saved. (Col 1:18)

4. **Q.** What is the overall purpose of the church?
   A. The church is the birth canal for spiritual conception and is therefore

charged with the nurturing and spiritual growth and development of its members. (Eph 4:14, Romans 5:14, 1 Thess 5:11, 1Cor 11:23-26)

5. **Q. How does the church differ from the house of Israel?**
   A. Israel is the wife of Jehovah while the church is the wife of Jesus. The church is filled with the Spirit of Christ and will therefore join Him in the rapture as the wise virgins. As the foolish virgins, Israel is blind to that wisdom and will not join the Lord when He returns in the air. When Jehovah and Jesus are consummated back to the unique spiritual unity, then the church and Israel will also become one. (Rev. 21:1, 2, 12, 14, Matt 25:1, 2, 1Cor. 15:28)

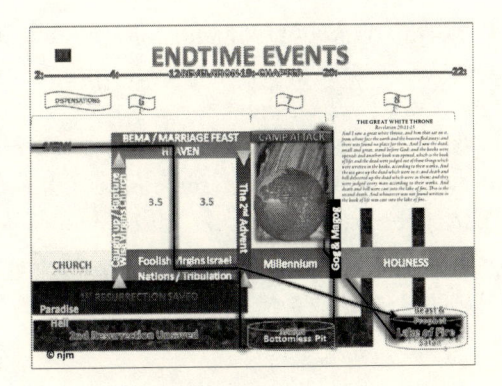

The Rapture

And if I go and prepare a place for you, I will come again, and receive you unto myself; that where I am, there ye may be also.
John 14:3

For the Lord himself shall descend from heaven with a shout, with the voice of the archangel, and with the trump of God: and the dead in Christ shall rise first: Then we which are alive and remain shall be caught up together with them in the clouds, to meet the Lord in the air: and so shall we ever be with the Lord.
1 Thessalonians 4:16-17

Behold, I shew you a mystery; We shall not all sleep, but we shall all be changed, In a moment, in the twinkling of an eye, at the last trump: for the trumpet shall sound, and the dead shall be raised incorruptible, and we shall be changed. For this corruptible must put on incorruption, and this mortal must put on immortality. So when this corruptible shall have put on incorruption, and this mortal shall have put on immortality, then shall be brought to pass the saying that is written, Death is swallowed up in victory. O death, where is thy sting? O grave, where is thy victory? The sting of death is sin; and the strength of sin is the law. But thanks be to God, which giveth us the victory through our Lord Jesus Christ. Therefore, my beloved brethren, be ye stedfast, unmoveable, always abounding in the work of the

Lord, forasmuch as ye know that your labour is not in vain in the Lord. **1 Corinthians 15:51-58**

But let us, who are of the day, be sober, putting on the breastplate of faith and love; and for an helmet, the hope of salvation. For God hath not appointed us to wrath, but to obtain salvation by our Lord Jesus Christ, Who died for us, that, whether we wake or sleep, we should live together with him.
1 Thessalonians 5:8-10

After this I looked, and, behold, a door was opened in heaven: and the first voice which I heard was as it were of a trumpet talking with me; which said, Come up hither, and I will shew thee things which must be hereafter.
Revelation 4:1

QUESTIONS AND ANSWERS

The Rapture

1. Q. When the Rapture comes, who will be able to go to heaven?
   A. The church, which consists of all who are born again. (John 3:5)

2. Q. What will happen to the children when the Lord returns?
   A. All Children under the age of accountability will be raptured. (Matthew 19:14)

3. Q. Will the children of all nations be raptured or just the children of Christians?
   A. Children of all nations, tongues, kindreds, and people will be raptured. (John 10:27, 28)

4. Q. Will unborn infants be afforded personal identification and circumstances?
   A. No, Infants that are unborn are subject to the conditions of their mother. (Matt 24:19, 1 Cor. 7:14, Jer. 1:5)

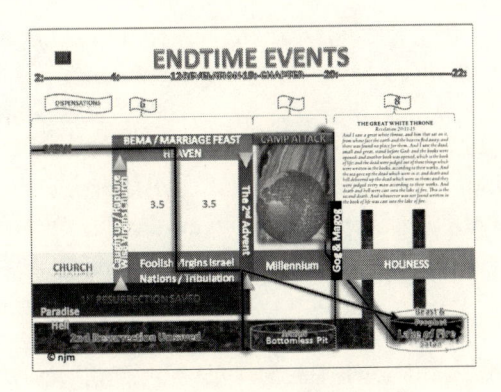

The Tribulation

The great tribulation - And I said unto him, Sir, thou knowest. And he said to me, These are they which came out of great tribulation, and have washed their robes, and made them white in the blood of the Lamb. **Revelation 7:14**

The time of distress - And at that time shall Michael stand up, the great prince which standeth for the children of thy people: and there shall be a time of trouble, such as never was since there was a nation even to that same time: and at that time thy people shall be delivered, every one that shall be found written in the book. **Daniel 12:1**

The great distress- For then shall be great tribulation, such as was not since the beginning of the world to this time, no, nor ever shall be. **Matthew 24:21** (See also Mat 24:21, Mark 13:19 and Luke 21:20-24)

The time of anguish and perplexity - And there shall be signs in the sun, and in the moon, and in the stars; and upon the earth distress of nations, with perplexity; the sea and the waves roaring; **Luke 21:25**

The man of lawlessness - Let no man deceive you by any means:

for that day shall not come, except there come a falling away first, and that man of sin be revealed, the son of perdition;
2 Thessalonians 2:3

The hour of trial - *Because thou hast kept the word of my patience, I also will keep thee from the hour of temptation, which shall come upon all the world, to try them that dwell upon the earth.*
Revelation 3:10

God's Covenant with Israel - *Ye stand this day all of you before the LORD your God; your captains of your tribes, your elders, and your officers, with all the men of Israel, Your little ones, your wives, and thy stranger that is in thy camp, from the hewer of thy wood unto the drawer of thy water: That thou shouldest enter into covenant with the LORD thy God, and into his oath, which the LORD thy God maketh with thee this day: That he may establish thee to day for a people unto himself, and that he may be unto thee a God, as he hath said unto thee, and as he hath sworn unto thy fathers, to Abraham, to Isaac, and to Jacob. Neither with you only do I make this covenant and this oath; But with him that standeth here with us this day before the LORD our God, and also with him that is not here with us this day: (For ye know how we have dwelt in the land of Egypt; and how we came through the nations which ye passed by; And ye have seen their abominations, and their idols, wood and stone, silver and gold, which were among them:)*
Deuteronomy 29:10-17

Lest there should be among you man, or woman, or family, or tribe, whose heart turneth away this day from the LORD our God, to go and serve the gods of these nations; lest there should be among you a root that beareth gall and wormwood; And it come to pass, when he heareth the words of this curse, that he bless himself in his heart, saying, I shall have peace, though I walk in the imagination of mine heart, to add drunkenness to thirst: The LORD will not spare him, but then the anger of the LORD and his jealousy shall smoke against that man, and all the curses that are written in this book shall lie upon him, and the LORD shall blot out his name from under heaven. And the LORD shall separate him unto evil out of all the tribes of Israel, according to all the curses of the covenant that are written in this book of the law: So that the generation to come of your children that shall rise up after you, and the stranger that shall come from a far land, shall say, when they see the plagues of that land, and the sicknesses which the LORD hath laid upon it; And that the whole land thereof is brimstone, and salt, and burning, that it is not sown, nor beareth, nor any grass groweth therein, like the overthrow of Sodom, and Gomorrah, Admah, and Zeboim, which the LORD overthrew in his anger, and in his wrath: Even all nations shall say, Wherefore hath the LORD done thus unto this land? What meaneth the heat of this great anger?

Deuteronomy 29:18-24

Then men shall say, Because they have forsaken the covenant of the LORD God of their fathers, which he made with them when he brought them forth out of the land of Egypt: For they went and served other gods, and worshipped them, gods whom they knew not, and whom he had not given unto them: And the anger of the LORD was kindled against this land, to bring upon it all the curses that are written in this book: And the LORD rooted them out of their land in anger, and in wrath, and in great indignation, and cast them into another land, as it is this day. The secret things belong unto the LORD our God: but those things which are revealed belong unto us and to our children for ever, that we may do all the words of this law.

Deuteronomy 29:25-29

Israel's violation of the covenant -*Then Jeroboam built Shechem in mount Ephraim, and dwelt therein; and went out from thence, and built Penuel. And Jeroboam said in his heart, Now shall the kingdom return to the house of David: If this people go up to do sacrifice in the house of the LORD at Jerusalem, then shall the heart of this people turn again unto their lord, even unto Rehoboam king of Judah, and they shall kill me, and go again to Rehoboam king of Judah. Whereupon the king took counsel, and made two calves of gold, and said unto them, It is too much* *for you to go up to Jerusalem: behold thy gods, O Israel, which brought thee up out of the land of Egypt. And he set the one in Bethel, and the other put he in Dan. And this thing became a sin: for the people went to worship before the one, even unto Dan.*

1 Kings 12:25-30

QUESTIONS AND ANSWERS
The Tribulation

1. Q. Will there be a great number of murders during the tribulation?
   A. Yes, as many as 2/3rds of the people will suffer death. (Zec. 13:8)

2. Q. Is the Tribulation about God's wrath, or His Glory?
   A. Both. God decreed to His people that they would inherit His wrath for apostasy, and His Grace for obedience. (**Deuteronomy 29:25-29**)

3. Q. Will people who practice other religious doctrines during the Tribulation have the opportunity to be saved?
   A. Yes. If such ones are brought to the realization that Jesus is God and that Christianity is the only true religion. They will come to this realization due, in part, to the sudden disappearance of children along with the mighty evangelical missions led by Moses, Elijah and the angels. (Rev 14:6-11)

4. Q. Will those who did have the opportunity to embrace the gospel be saved if they are left at the time of the rapture?
   A. No, those who had the opportunity to accept Jesus but refused His invitation will be lost. (2 Thess 2:7-12)

5. Q. How can we be sure that the church will not go through the Tribulation?
   A. The greatest assurance lies in the fact that the Tribulation is brought on by the Lord Himself. Why would He subject His body to His

wrath when He clearly speaks personal peace to His church? The church is the body and bride of Christ. For her to encounter the tribulation would mean that Jesus would have to suffer again at His own hand. (Heb 6:6, Heb 9:23-28, Rev 3:10)

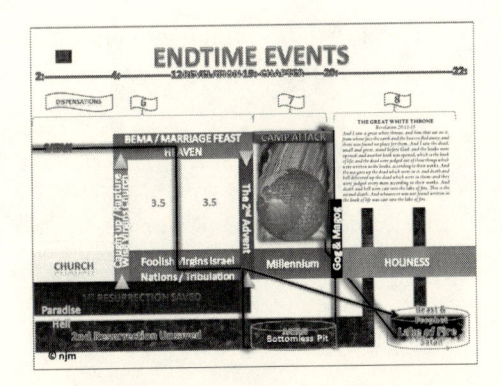

BEMA JUDGMENT

For we must all appear before the judgment seat of Christ; that every one may receive the things done in his body, according to that he hath done, whether it be good or bad.
2 Corinthians 5:10

Incorruptible "Crown of Salvation" - *And every man that striveth for the mastery is temperate in all things. Now they do it to obtain a corruptible crown; but we an incorruptible.*
1Corinthians 9:25

Living "Martyrs Crown" - *Fear none of those things which thou shalt suffer: behold, the devil shall cast some of you into prison, that ye may be tried; and ye shall have tribulation ten days: be thou faithful unto death, and I will give thee a crown of life.*
Revelation 2:10

Glory "Pastor's Crown" - *Feed the flock of God which is among you, taking the oversight thereof, not by constraint, but willingly; not for filthy lucre, but of a ready mind; Neither as being lords over God's heritage, but being ensamples to the flock. And when the chief Shepherd shall appear, ye shall receive a crown of glory that fadeth not away.* **1 Peter 5:2-4**

Righteousness "Crown of Faith" - *Henceforth there is laid up for me a crown of righteousness, which the Lord, the righteous* *judge, shall give me at that day: and not to me only, but unto all them also that love his appearing.* **2Timothy 4:8**

Rejoicing "Soul Winner's Crown *"For what is our hope, or joy, or crown of rejoicing? Are not even ye in the presence of our Lord Jesus Christ at his coming? For ye are our glory and joy.*
1Thessalonians 2:19, 20

QUESTIONS AND ANSWERS
Bema Judgment

1. Q. **Is the BEMA a biblical term?**
   A   No, the term BEMA represents an Olympic judgment of winners. The Church will encounter a judgment of works where each member will receive due recognition for the works done in the flesh.
   2 Corinthians 5:10

2. Q. **Is the BEMA the only judgment that Christians will encounter.**
   A   No, In order to qualify for the BEMA judgment you must be born again. Being born again requires one to have been judged of sin, and justified by the saving grace of Jesus Christ. The Christian experiences two judgments. The first of sin, and the last of works
   John 3:3

3. Q   Since the BEMA literally means "base or foot" implying a raised seat, such as the judge's bench, is it conceivable that this judgment will include curses also?
   A   No, The saints of God shall be relieved of all conditions that would otherwise inhibit. Paul spoke of this judgment as a fiery trial, where the unacceptable works were consumed, yet the person was not.
   1 Corinthians 3:13-15

4. Q   Does the advocating of a BEMA judgment conflict with the doctrine of grace?
   A   No, grace is the key to heaven, yet the convert is still under their personal will to obey the Lord's Spiritual leadership. Paul spoke of

himself as a possible reprobate except he continued in the Lord's will." *But I keep under my body, and bring it into subjection: lest that by any means, when I have preached to others, I myself should be a castaway. 1Corinthians 9:27"* **Paul** was not questioning his salvation (2Corinthians 12:9), but the benefits of his judgment. When reading the above scriptures representing the five mentioned crowns, take note of the accompanying conditions for each award. In short we have unconditional salvation but conditional rewards.
Heb. 13:17...1Peter 4:5, 6

5. **Q** If we are going to be judged at the BEMA wouldn't our judgment honor ourselves rather than Christ?

    No, The Lord through the power of the Holy Spirit provokes us to His will, yet the spirit of the prophet is subject to the prophet (1Corinthians 14:32) therefore man must give account for the things that are done in the flesh. In the book of James chapter 2, the Apostle goes into great detail explaining the conditions of faith and works. Some believe James to be in conflict with Paul when it comes to whether a person is saved of faith or works. Paul stressed the former while James seemingly the latter. James was not disagreeing with the means of salvation he was accentuating the judgment of works. In other words when a person gets saved they should get busy. Paul the champion of salvation strictly by faith wrote; "*Wherefore, my beloved, as ye have always obeyed, not as in my presence only, but now much more in my absence, work out your own salvation with fear and trembling. Philippians 2:12*"

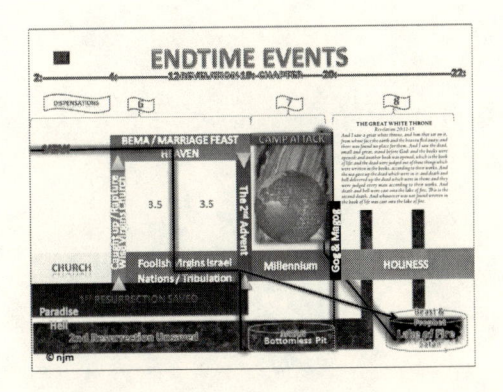

The Marriage Feast

The kingdom of heaven is like unto a certain king, which made a marriage for his son, **Matthew 22:2**

And while they went to buy, the bridegroom came; and they that were ready went in with him to the marriage: and the door was shut. **Matthew 25:10**

Let us be glad and rejoice, and give honour to him: for the marriage of the Lamb is come, and his wife hath made herself ready. And to her was granted that she should be arrayed in fine linen, clean and white: for the fine linen is the righteousness of saints. And he saith unto me, Write, Blessed are they which are called unto the marriage supper of the Lamb. And he saith unto me, These are the true sayings of God. **Revelation 19:7-9**

QUESTIONS AND ANSWERS
The Marriage Feast

1. Q. How will the church be judged?
   A. The church will be judged for its works. The first work is the work of salvation, termed the incorruptible crown. Paul explained to the Corinthians that every man's work will be tried as by fire. Although there will certainly be inadequacies in works, the saint will not be destroyed. (1 Corinthians 3:13-15)

2. Q. Will those who die for the Lord during the Tribulation become a part of the church in the Bema?
   A. No, the souls of those who are killed during the tribulation for the cause of Christ are seen under the alter of God and will receive their resurrected bodies at the 1st resurrection. (Rev 20:4)

3. Q. Will the souls of those that are killed during the tribulation for professing Jesus as their Saviour become a part of the church in heaven?
   A. No. They are the guest at the marriage feast and will not receive their resurrected bodies until the Lords return. (Matt 22:11, Rev 6:11, Rev 20:6)

4. Q. Will the Jews become a part of the church during the marriage feast of the lamb?
   A. No. The Jews will receive their earthly Kingdom with the Lord, (the offspring of David) during Jesus' millennial reign. After which all

those who are identified as lambs will be translated and become one in New Jerusalem. (Rev 21:2)

5. **Q. Will there ever be a time when the Jews and the church will consummate their holy relationship?**
   A. Yes. After the millennium, the consummated body of the Lord is referred to as New Jerusalem. She is seen descending out of heaven to a new earth after the millennium. . She is represented by the house of Israel in her gates and the church in her foundation. Gal. 3: 27-29, (Rev 21: 1, 2)

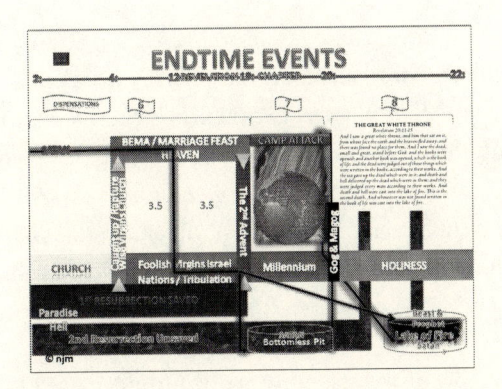

The 2nd Advent of the Lord

And I saw heaven opened, and behold a white horse; and he that sat upon him was called Faithful and True, and in righteousness he doth judge and make war. His eyes were as a flame of fire, and on his head were many crowns; and he had a name written, that no man knew, but he himself. And he was clothed with a vesture dipped in blood: and his name is called The Word of God. And the armies which were in heaven followed him upon white horses, clothed in fine linen, white and clean. And out of his mouth goeth a sharp sword, that with it he should smite the nations: and he shall rule them with a rod of iron: and he treadeth the winepress of the fierceness and wrath of Almighty God. And he hath on his vesture and on his thigh a name written, KING OF KINGS, AND LORD OF LORDS. **Revelation 19:11-16**

And he gathered them together into a place called in the Hebrew tongue Armageddon. **Revelation 16:16**

And the beast was taken, and with him the false prophet that wrought miracles before him, with which he deceived them that had received the mark of the beast, and them that worshipped his image. These both were cast alive into a lake of fire burning with brimstone. And the remnant were slain with the sword of him that sat upon the horse, which sword proceeded out of his mouth: and all the fowls were filled with their flesh.
Revelation 19:20-21

And I saw an angel come down from heaven, having the key of the bottomless pit and a great chain in his hand. And he laid hold on the dragon, that old serpent, which is the Devil, and Satan, and bound him a thousand years, Revelation 20:3 And cast him into the bottomless pit, and shut him up, and set a seal upon him, that he should deceive the nations no more, till the thousand years should be fulfilled: and after that he must be loosed a little season. **Revelation 20:1-2**

When the Son of man shall come in his glory, and all the holy angels with him, then shall he sit upon the throne of his glory: And before him shall be gathered all nations: and he shall separate them one from another, as a shepherd divideth his sheep from the goats: **Matthew 25:31-32**

But the rest of the dead lived not again until the thousand years were finished. This is the first resurrection. Blessed and holy is he that hath part in the first resurrection: on such the second death hath no power, but they shall be priests of God and of Christ, and shall reign with him a thousand years. **Revelation 20:5-6**

QUESTION AND ANSWER

The Second Advent

1. **Q. When Jesus returns, will He display vengeance or wrath?**
   A. Yes, He will display both. The Lord's vengeance and wrath is seen in the blood of His enemies on His vesture. (Rev 19:13, Isa 63:1-6)

2. **Q. Will the Lord's return affect the power of sin?**
   A. Yes. The unholy trio of Satan, the Antichrist, and the False prophet will be removed from the presence of the people for a season during which no one will die. (Rev 19:20, 20:1,2)

3. **Q. Will there be a resurrection when the Lord returns?**
   A. Yes. It is called the first resurrection. It will involve all the saints who died or were killed during the tribulation. (Rev 20:4,5)

4. **Q. Will there also be a resurrection of the unsaved when the Lord returns to judge the nations?**
   A. No. The resurrection of the unsaved will occur at the end of the Millennium and is called the Second Resurrection. This resurrection will render the dead not of Christ back into bodies of flesh, to be judged in damnation and killed a second time. The second death will render these souls into the Lake of Fire for all eternity. Thus none will be saved in this resurrection. (Rev 20:6, 13, Daniel 12:2, John 5:29)

5. Q. **When Jesus returns to judge the nations, will some be condemned to death and others to life?**
   A. Yes, this event is referred to as "The Judgment of the Nations" or "The Judgment of the Sheep and the Goats". (Matt. 25:31-46)

6. Q. **Will the unsaved be killed?**
   A. Yes. They will be cast into hell (grave) while the beast and the false prophet go into the Lake of Fire. (Rev 19:21) In the final judgment (White Throne) death and hell will be cast into the Lake of Fire. Revelation 20:14

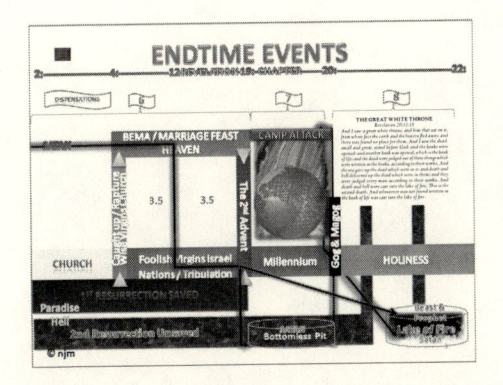

The Millennium Kingdom (1,000 years)

Thy kingdom come. Thy will be done in earth, as it is in heaven.
Matthew 6:10

Blessed and holy is he that hath part in the first resurrection: on such the second death hath no power, but they shall be priests of God and of Christ, and shall reign with him a thousand years.
Revelation 20:6

But with righteousness shall he judge the poor, and reprove with equity for the meek of the earth: and he shall smite the earth with the rod of his mouth, and with the breath of his lips shall he slay the wicked. And righteousness shall be the girdle of his loins, and faithfulness the girdle of his reins. The wolf also shall dwell with the lamb, and the leopard shall lie down with the kid; and the calf and the young lion and the fatling together; and a little child shall lead them. And the cow and the bear shall feed; their young ones shall lie down together: and the lion shall eat straw like the ox. And the sucking child shall play on the hole of the asp, and the weaned child shall put his hand on the cockatrice' den. They shall not hurt nor destroy in all my holy mountain: for the earth shall be full of the knowledge of the LORD, as the waters cover the sea.
Isaiah 11:4-9

QUESTION AND ANSWER
The Millennium Kingdom

1. Q. **Are the Jews expecting the Lord to return to earth and set up His kingdom?**
   A. Yes. The Jews were anticipating the fulfillment of the prophesy of Malachi concerning the return of Elijah as the forerunner of Christ. They questioned John the Baptist and also the very presence of Christ trying to confirm Elijah's return. When they were unsuccessful in the confirmation they resolved that Christ could not be the Messiah. (Mal 3:1, 4:5, 6, Isa 40:3, Zech 12:10-14, John 1:21-25, Mark 6:15, Luke 9:19)

2. Q. **Will King David ever again sit on the throne of Israel as prophesied in the book of Ezekiel?**

   > *"Ezekiel 37:25 And they shall dwell in the land that I have given unto Jacob my servant, wherein your fathers have dwelt; and they shall dwell therein, even they, and their children, and their children's children for ever: and my servant David shall be their prince for ever"*

   A. No. It is inappropriate to interpret the prophesy of the Kingdom of David as an eternal earthily kingdom. Notice that the scripture above references David as "their prince forever." If David is the prince, who is the King (*See* Rev 19:16, 1 Tim 6:15)? The answer is Jesus; the root (King) and offspring (prince) of David (Rev 22:16). In this instance, the earthily kingdom of David is but a representation of the heavenly kingdom of Christ. (Matt 6:10)

3. **Q. Should we understand the Millennium to be a literal 1,000 years?**
   A. Yes. The Millennial Kingdom is the title given to the 1000-year reign of Jesus Christ on the earth. Some seek to interpret the 1,000 years in an allegorical manner. Some understand the 1000 years as merely a figurative way of saying "a long period of time," not a literal, physical reign of Jesus Christ on the earth. Six times in Revelation 20:2-7, the Millennial Kingdom is explicitly stated as being 1,000 years in length. If God wished to communicate "a long period of time," He could have easily done so without repeatedly naming an exact time frame. (Revelation 20:2-7)

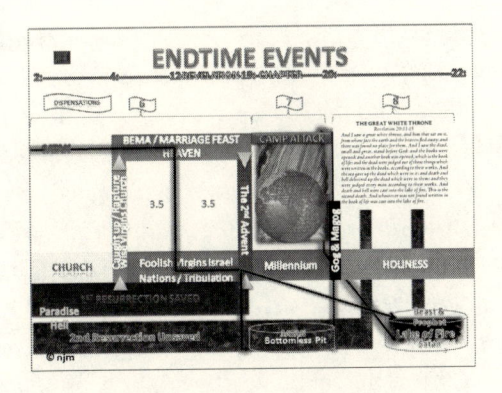

Gog and Magog

And when the thousand years are expired, Satan shall be loosed out of his prison, And shall go out to deceive the nations which are in the four quarters of the earth, Gog and Magog, to gather them together to battle: the number of whom is as the sand of the sea. And they went up on the breadth of the earth, and compassed the camp of the saints about, and the beloved city: and fire came down from God out of heaven, and devoured them. And the devil that deceived them was cast into the lake of fire and brimstone, where the beast and the false prophet are, and shall be tormented day and night for ever and ever.

Revelation 20:7-10

But the day of the Lord will come as a thief in the night; in the which the heavens shall pass away with a great noise, and the elements shall melt with fervent heat, the earth also and the works that are therein shall be burned up. Seeing then that all these things shall be dissolved, what manner of persons ought ye to be in all holy conversation and godliness, Looking for and hasting unto the coming of the day of God, wherein the heavens being on fire shall be dissolved, and the elements shall melt with fervent heat? Nevertheless we, according to his promise, look for new heavens and a new earth, wherein dwelleth righteousness.

2 Peter 3:10-13

And I saw a great white throne, and him that sat on it, from whose face the earth and the heaven fled away; and there was found no place for them. And I saw the dead, small and great, stand before God; and the books were opened: and another book was opened, which is the book of life: and the dead were judged out of those things which were written in the books, according to their works. And the sea gave up the dead which were in it; and death and hell delivered up the dead which were in them: and they were judged every man according to their works. And death and hell were cast into the lake of fire. This is the second death. And whosoever was not found written in the book of life was cast into the lake of fire. **Revelation 20:11-1**

QUESTION AND ANSWER
Gog and Magog

1. **Q. What is the significance of the term "Gog and Magog"?**
   A. Historically speaking, Magog was a grandson of Noah (Genesis 10:2). The descendants of Magog settled to the far north of Israel, likely in Europe and northern Asia (Ezekiel 38:2). Magog seems to be used to refer to "northern barbarians" in general, but likely also has a connection to Magog the person. The people of Magog are described as skilled warriors by Ezekiel. Gog was a great warrior defeated by God. (Ezek 38:2, 3; 38:15; 39:3-9)

2. **Q. Is the Gog and Magog in the book of Revelation connected to the Gog and Magog of Ezekiel's time?**
   A. The duplicated use of the name Gog and Magog in Revelation 20:8-9 is to show that these people demonstrate the same rebellion against God and antagonism toward God as those in Ezekiel 38-39. It is similar to someone today calling a person "the devil" because he or she is sinful and evil. We know that person is not really Satan, but because that person shares similar characteristics, he or she might be referred to as "the devil".

3. **Q. Does the presence of the kingdom of Israel have any meaning to Gog and Magog?**
   A. The battle in Ezekiel 38-39 is used by God to bring Israel back to Him (Ezekiel 39:21-29). In Revelation chapter 20, Israel has been faithful to God for 1,000 years (the millennial kingdom). Those in Revelation 20:7-10 who are rebellious are destroyed without any

more opportunity for repentance. In the prophetical sense Gog and Magog represent the final emancipation of humanity from the assaults of Satan and his evil cohorts. (Revelation 20:8)

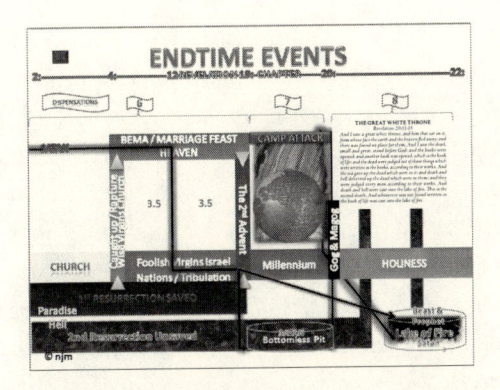

The Great White Throne Judgment
The Dispensation of Holiness

But now is Christ risen from the dead, and become the firstfruits of them that slept. For since by man came death, by man came also the resurrection of the dead. For as in Adam all die, even so in Christ shall all be made alive. But every man in his own order: Christ the firstfruits; afterward they that are Christ's at his coming. Then cometh the end, when he shall have delivered up the kingdom to God, even the Father; when he shall have put down all rule and all authority and power. For he must reign, till he hath put all enemies under his feet. The last enemy that shall be destroyed is death. For he hath put all things under his feet. But when he saith all things are put under him, it is manifest that he is excepted, which did put all things under him. And when all things shall be subdued unto him, then shall the Son also himself be subject unto him that put all things under him, that God may be all in all. **1 Corinthians 15:20-28**

And I saw a new heaven and a new earth: for the first heaven and the first earth were passed away; and there was no more sea. And I John saw the holy city, new Jerusalem, coming down from God out of heaven, prepared as a bride adorned for her husband. And I heard a great voice out of heaven saying, Behold, the tabernacle of God is with men, and he will dwell with them, and they shall be his people, and God himself shall be with them, and be their God. And God shall wipe away all tears from their

eyes; and there shall be no more death, neither sorrow, nor crying, neither shall there be any more pain: for the former things are passed away. And he that sat upon the throne said, Behold, I make all things new. And he said unto me, Write: for these words are true and faithful. And he said unto me, It is done. I am Alpha and Omega, the beginning and the end. I will give unto him that is athirst of the fountain of the water of life freely. He that overcometh shall inherit all things; and I will be his God, and he shall be my son. But the fearful, and unbelieving, and the abominable, and murderers, and whoremongers, and sorcerers, and idolaters, and all liars, shall have their part in the lake which burneth with fire and brimstone: which is the second death.
Revelation 21:1-8

And he shewed me a pure river of water of life, clear as crystal, proceeding out of the throne of God and of the Lamb. In the midst of the street of it, and on either side of the river, was there the tree of life, which bare twelve manner of fruits, and yielded her fruit every month: and the leaves of the tree were for the healing of the nations. And there shall be no more curse: but the throne of God and of the Lamb shall be in it; and his servants shall serve him: And they shall see his face; and his name shall be in their foreheads. And there shall be no night there; and they need no candle, neither light of the sun; for the Lord God giveth them light: and they shall reign for ever and ever.
Revelation 22:1-5

He which testifieth these things saith, Surely I come quickly. Amen. Even so, come, Lord Jesus. The grace of our Lord Jesus Christ be with you all. Amen.   **Revelation 22:20-21**

QUESTIONS AND ANSWERS

The White Throne Judgment

1. Q. Revelation 20:11-15 speaks of the White Throne Judgment, what is significant about it?
   A. When a convicted person returns to court for sentencing there is no possible expectation of being released. The White Throne judgment is the eternal sentencing hearing before Jesus Christ. This remarkable passage introduces to us the final judgment—the end of human history and the beginning of the eternal state. (Revelation 20:13)

2. Q. Will the judge be God the Father or Jesus the Christ?
   A. Paul assured Timothy (2 Timothy 4:1-8) that the Lord Jesus Christ will be the judge of all. Isaiah spoke (33:22) of the judgment of the "Lord". The righteous judge is none other than Jesus Christ. He is identified during His return by the insignia "King of Kings and Lord of Lords" (Rev. 19:16). The Bible is very clear that unbelievers are storing up wrath against themselves (Romans 2:5) and that God will "give to each person according to what he has done" (Romans 2:6). To the Romans Paul spoke of the judgment of God, yet to Timothy he spoke of the judgment of Jesus Christ. Again that which could appear conflicting is not since Jesus and God are the same. Jesus Christ is the only image of the Spirit / invisible God. (1Timothy 6:15, 16) In the final analysis the bible makes it crystal clear that God the Father judges no man, the honor belongs solely to Jesus. (John 5:22, 23)

3. Q. Does this judgment involve all people, saved and unsaved?
   A. No. This is the seventh and last judgment and all who are saved

would have already received a judgment of faith and of works. The first judgment is the judgment of sin. Jesus redeems the church by repentance, conversion, and regeneration. Having received Jesus the believer is only to anticipate the BEMA judgment of works. The White Throne judgment is a sentencing of those that refused Jesus during their life-time. (John 5:29)

4. **Q. What are the seven judgments of humanity?**
   A. The seven judgments date back from the events in the Garden of Eden to the future events revealed in the Revelation. Through the sin of Adam and Eve all of humanity was judged sinful. Following the acts of the inaugural family God required sacrifice. Cain was judged to be disobedient because he did not give God his first. Such sacrifices continued until Jesus came and made the ultimate sacrifice for the sins of the world. After Jesus' ascension to Heaven, the Holy Spirit established the "You Testament", the opportunity for all to confess their sins through repentance and to be judged righteous by the blood of Jesus. The saved, "church" will be caught up to be with the Lord in heaven at His return. It will be there in heaven that the church will encounter its judgment of works "The BEMA". During the same period of time that the church is being judged in heaven the House of Israel will be judged in earth. When the Lord returns to earth following the Tribulation He will judge the Nations "Gentiles" and set up His Millennium kingdom here on earth as it is in heaven. Following the Millennium kingdom all of those that refused God will be resurrected to a sentencing judgment proclaimed "The white Throne Judgment."

The seven judgments

1. *Judgment of Obedience*.................... *Eden*.. *Gen 3:2, 3*
2. *Judgment of Sacrifice* .... *Law* .... *Numbers 27:12-14*
3. *Judgment Of Grace*.......................... *World*............................... *Matt 28:19, 20*
4. *Judgment of Church*........................ *Bema*........................... *2Corinthians 5:10*
5. *Judgment of the Nations* .... *Gentiles*................................. *Matt 25:31*
6. *Judgment of Tribulation*................. *Israel* .... *Deut. 29:21*
7. *Judgment of Sins*............................. *White Throne* .... *Rev. 20:11, 12*

The thief cometh not, but for to steal, and to kill, and to destroy: I am come that they might have life, and that they might have it more abundantly.

JOHN 10:10

EPILOG
"Is It All About Love?"

Contrary to popular belief, sin was already well in existence before the creation of man. The books of Isaiah and Ezekiel reveal that Lucifer was in the Garden of Eden before it was made habitable for humanity.[197] Adam's creation was the answer to the already existing problem of sin. He was created from the dust of the earth to defeat Lucifer, the highest order of God's creation[198]. The archangel had surrendered his premier seat in the angelic hierarchy due to his own vaulting pride and desire to be like God.[199]

The book of Genesis states that in the beginning God created the Heavens and the Earth; so the beginning of creation is obviously the first estate of matter.[200] Based on what we know of God's characteristics, surely nothing done by Him is incomplete[201]. Therefore, the original creation must have been perfect in every way. However, in seemingly contrast, the second verse of Genesis chapter one says that the earth was void. We will now address the mystery behind the reason for this darkness[202] for we are certain that God is light and in Him dwelled nothing dark.

We are given a beautiful depiction of the earth prior to the introduction of sin. The holy host of angels walked among mountains of fire and praised God on this very earth.[203] These mountains were the precious stones that many today work so hard to afford. Diamonds, rubies, emeralds, jade, silver,

---

197 Isaiah 14:12-20 Ezekiel 28:13-15
198 Ezekiel 28:14-15
199 Isaiah 14: 12-17
200 Genesis 1:1
201 Matthew 11:11
202 Isaiah 14:17
203 Ezekiel 28:14

gold, onyx, sapphire and countless other precious stones layered the earth.[204] No dirt or dust; everything clean, bright, and brilliantly glowing to the glory of God. They were so beautiful, so powerful in existence until the temptation overcame Lucifer to go beyond that of steward and attempt to overthrow God and own it.[205]

Satan recruited other angels to carry out a coup to takeover God's government. When God cast him into the earth[206] He caused an implosion and an explosion. Envision the falling mountains of gold, silver, diamonds and other precious stones that are now buried under the core. Imagine seeing some of this beautiful substance flying out into the universe and settling into what we now call the solar system.

In an instant, Satan lost a beautiful world and inherited this dusty earth. He lost eternal favor and inherited damnation. No longer the guardian of truth and light, he is now the ruler of darkness; the father of every lie and the author of the second death.[207] Satan had made a fatal mistake in challenging his maker. He wanted his own government, so God gave him the authority to claim one. Armed with deceit and lies, Satan took the kingdom that God had given to Adam and Eve. While he is referred to by several different names and titles, i.e. Lucifer, Devil, serpent, and god of this world, Satan is the name that reveals his core character; devil, evil spirit, adversary. How fitting indeed.

The now bruised and battered archangel watched enviously as the Power of God, "The Holy Spirit", moved to renovate the remaining earth for the habitation of man. Imagine Satan's confusion as he observed the restoration and second state of the earth. Man was an unknown to Satan, existing only in the mind of God. Unlike Satan, man was created weak and finite, clothed in dirt and subject to the elements[208]. Faith was also an unknown to Satan; he hoped for nothing.[209]

Comparatively, both angels and humanity were given a free will. As intelligent beings, we can acknowledge God's praiseworthiness by willfully worshipping Him. Because the creature is not forced to worship the Creator, worship by the creature should be sincere worship. Such sincerity could not

---

204 Ezekiel 28:13
205 Ezekiel 28:17
206 Luke 10:18
207 1 John 3:8; 5:18; John 8:44; 10:10
208 Ezekiel 28:15
209 Ezekiel 28:15

be accomplished in the absence of free will. Satan was the first creation to exercise free will in opposition to the Creator. From the loftiest position in God's kingdom he sought to rise above God.

Adam, who was given only one law, "*of the tree of the knowledge of good and evil, thou shalt not eat of it*",[210] was nonetheless, also challenged due to the gift of free will. The tree represented the will of God and the obedience of man. The family had the choice of obeying or rejecting God's will. Any and every decision to go against the will of God ultimately results in death. The devil is the father of sin and all who follow him are subject to the same destiny; death.[211] Satan, however was altogether unaware that his evil devices had already been factored into God's plan. Man was created as a display of God's love. This love would be magnified through the fall and apparent defeat of human-kind.

The regenerated world would now contain beings capable of reproducing their kind.[212] The bond established in this connection was proven unbreakable by Adam's response to Eve's wrongdoing. Adam's love for her perfectly mirrors God's love for mankind. His failure to refrain from the tree was in no way related to any desire in himself to become like God. He did not eat to become great. Adam ate to remain with his bride. He knew full well what the outcome of this transgression would be. Adam made a conscious decision not to have Eve cast out of the garden alone. Adam found himself faced with the decision of whether to follow Eve or allow her to face her demise alone. Somehow Adam found in God's instructions the responsibility to protect her at all cost. His love was proven by his sacrifice. God would later assign to Himself the spiritual title of 'Adam' as His sacrifice for mankind proved a much higher love.[213]

> *And Adam was not deceived, but the woman being deceived was in the transgression. Notwithstanding she shall be saved in childbearing, if they continue in faith and charity and holiness with sobriety.* 1 Timothy 2:14-15

> *And so it is written, The first man Adam was made a living soul; the last Adam was made a quickening spirit.*
> 1 Corinthians 15:45

---

210 Genesis 2:17
211 Romans 6:16
212 Genesis 2:21-23
213 1Corinthians 15:45

Adam's display of love for his otherwise cast away wife earned him the distinction "first Adam". Significantly, Jesus is referred to as the last Adam.[214] Just as Adam made the ultimate sacrifice for Eve, Jesus would do the same for His bride, the Church.

Again, it should be emphasized that Adam's act was motivated by love and not greed.[215] The bible says that love will cover a multitude of sins; however, here it only needed to cover one, the transgression of Adam's wife.[216] Adam knew the consequence, yet the sacrificial nature of love compelled him to follow his wife into exile.[217] Yes, as noble as Adam was, the sting of sin is death and therefore it was *"appointed unto man once to die"*.[218]

But just as Adam left Eden to protect Eve, Jesus left heaven to protect *His* bride, the church. Christ loved her so much that He voluntarily gave up His "Eden" in heaven and became clothed in flesh; yet without sin.[219] His love is sacrificial. For us, He desired life; for Himself, He embraced death. In Eden, God made the first sacrifice when He took the life of an animal to clothe and protect the couple from the elements in their newly sinful state.[220] Yes, from the beginning, God's love made the appropriate sacrifice for mankind. In the end, He sacrificed Himself, delivering a fatal blow to the authority of Satan.[221]

As you can see, the war is between Satan and God.[222] All of the created beings of God will either follow Satan or Christ. To deny Christ is to accept Satan. To deny Satan, however, does not automatically qualify as having accepted Christ. This is due to the most important will in your life; your own.[223] God's will must outweigh even the personal will of the one who is to become His.[224]

---

214 Romans 5:14; 1 Corinthians 15:45
215 1 Timothy 2:14
216 1Peter 4:8
217 Luke 22:42
218 Hebrew 9:27
219 John 1:14; 3:16; Romans 5:8
220 Genesis 3:21 Unto Adam also and to his wife did the LORD God make coats of skins, and clothed them.
221 John 19:30 When Jesus therefore had received the vinegar, he said, It is finished: and he bowed his head, and gave up the ghost.
222 Ephesians 6:12
223 1 Corinthians 2:11 For what man knoweth the things of a man, save the spirit of man which is in him? even so the things of God knoweth no man, but the Spirit of God.
224 Mark 8:34 And when he had called the people unto him with his disciples also, he said unto them, Whosoever will come after me, let him deny himself, and take up his cross, and follow me.

Being saved through the power of regeneration marries you into the body of Christ's bride, the Church.[225] He died for the Church; therefore she was ransomed out of the jail of time.[226] He covered her sin; therefore, she is accepted of God. He made her without spot or wrinkle; she is clothed and made ready for the marriage feast.[227]

N. Jerome McClain Sr.

---

225 Romans 8:14 For as many as are led by the Spirit of God, they are the sons of God.
226 Ephesians 5:25 Husbands, love your wives, even as Christ also loved the Church, and gave himself for it;
227 Revelation 19:7

INDEX

Symbols

1st Adam existence 4
2nd Adam existence 4

A

Abram's tithe 50
Adam's creation 117
Alpha 28, 29, 112
Archangel 118

B

baptism 19, 20, 21, 22, 23, 24, 26, 27, 28, 30, 32, 40, 48
baptized 4
Baptizo 21
belong solely to God 51
Bethel 50
blood and water 24
book of life 108
born-again 5, 15
Buddhists 14

C

Catholic 35
Catholic Church 35
children 10, 14, 23, 54, 58, 85, 87
church and Israel 70
church ordinances 19
Closed Communion 36, 37
confess 33
consubstantiation 35

conversion/regeneration 9, 47
Cyrus A. Weaver 22

D

dispensation 69
dogma 19
duty of the saved 41

E

ecumenical dispensation 69
Eden 50, 114, 117, 120
Episcopal 36
eschatology 69
Eternal Salvation 13
Eucharist 35
Experiential 45
Experiential Sanctification 13, 45

F

faithful steward 45
fall of man 52
favor from God 35
fervent heat 107
First Adam 120
foolish virgins 71

G

Gentiles 27
Gestation
    Physical vs. Spiritual 5
Godhead 27

the god of the earth 118
God's Covenant with Israel 86
God the Father 12
God the Holy 12
God the Son 12
Gog and Magog 107

H

Hasmonean dynasty 3
Homologeō 33
the house of the Lord 57

I

If I were hungry 55
infallibility, immutability, perfection 12
instant death 57
Is It All About Love? 117

J

Jacob's tithe 50
Jehovah 26, 28
Jesus Cadets International 44
joining the church 19
Judas, Ananias and Sapphira 57
Judgment
    Seven Judgments 114

L

Look at Salvation through Trifocals 12
Love, Obedience, and Works 47
Love of God 119

M

management 43
managers 45
the most important will in your life 120
mountains of fire 117
Muslims 14
mystery 117

N

Nicodemus 4, 24

O

offerings 49, 51, 53, 57, 58
Omega 28, 29, 112
Omniscient Creator 13
Open Communion 36

P

Paradise 11
parents 16, 58
Positional Sanctification 13
precede baptism 22

Q

Q and A
    Holiness 113

R

Rapture 68, 70
Regeneration 12
remembrance 32
repentance 15, 26, 27, 114
robbery
    Are you guilty? 49
ruler of darkness 118

S

sacrifice 120
sanctification 13
seats of honor 48
Second Adam 120
second death 108, 118
solar system 118
sprinkling and pouring 24
steward 43
stewardship 45, 47
symbolic 36
symbolism 23

T

talents
    Predetermined 11
ten virgins 70

the test of fire 48
the threefold ministry 48
the tithe
    What about it? 55
transgression 120
transubstantiation 35
tribulation 68, 69, 85, 114
true worship 118

U

Ulrich Zwingli 36
Ultimate Positional Sanctified 13

W

washing feet 40
What constitutes baptism? 21
What does God own? 43
What do you control? 44
What do you own? 44
What precedes Baptism? 21
White Throne Judgment 111, 113

Y

You Need Jesus 16

Table of Figures

Figure 1 Time to Decide vii
Figure 2 Spiritual Competence of the Soul 10
Figure 3 Spiritual Growth 48
Figure 4 End Time Events 68

Edwards Brothers Malloy
Thorofare, NJ USA
September 12, 2012